Weird, Wacky and Wild

GEORGIA TRIVIA

Stephanie Watson & Lisa Wojna

BLUE
BIKE
BOOKS

The Publisher: Blue Bike Books

Website: www.bluebikebooks.com

Library and Archives Canada Cataloguing in Publication

Watson, Stephanie, 1969–
  Georgia trivia : weird, wacky and wild /
  Stephanie Watson and Lisa Wojna.

Georgia Trivia

ISBN: 978-1-897278-44-4

  1. Georgia—Miscellanea. I. Wojna, Lisa, 1962– II. Title.

Project Director: Nicholle Carrière
Project Editor: Kathy van Denderen
Production: Jodene Draven, Alexander Luthor, Vicky Tricket
Cover Image: Photo courtesy of Stockbyte/Adobe Stock Photos (2008);
  Autumnal Valley in Gerogia
Illustrations: Patrick Hénaff, Roger Garcia, Peter Tyler, Roly Wood

We acknowledge the support of the Alberta Foundation for the Arts for our publishing program.

PC: P5

DEDICATION

To Ken, for following me on this crazy journey southward and for loving me enough to stick around, and for Jake, my sweet southern boy.

–Stephanie

ACKNOWLEDGMENTS

Thank you to my friends and family for putting up with my prolonged absences during the compilation of this book. I'm also grateful to the diligent writers and editors of the *New Georgia Encyclopedia*, whose work served as a wonderful guide-post to this state I thought I knew so well, but have found that I am only beginning to discover.

–Stephanie

Many thanks to our clever editor, who pieced together the work of two authors and did so seamlessly; to my co-author, Stephanie; and to my family—my husband Garry, sons Peter, Matthew and Nathan, daughter Melissa and granddaughter Jada. Without you, all this and anything else I do in my life would be meaningless.

–Lisa

CONTENTS

INTRODUCTION

I remember very vividly my first trip to Georgia: I was riding in a cab down the mansion-lined streets of Buckhead, Atlanta's most elegant neighborhood, when I told the driver that I was thinking of relocating here from New Jersey. He peered at me in the rearview mirror, smiled slyly and drawled, "Well, you'll make a fine Georgia peach."

Yankee snob that I was back then, I couldn't envision calling Georgia home. Now, 14 years later, I have become wildly attached to this place, and I can hardly imagine living anywhere else, much less returning to my northern roots. Although I might not have transformed into the perfect southern belle, I have gained a real appreciation for the state I now call home.

There are so many things to love about Georgia, from the southern hospitality of its small towns to the worldly sophistication of its big cities. I love that men refer to me respectfully as "ma'am" without making me feel ancient and that I can get a slice of the best warm pecan pie in the universe. I also love that I can go see a concert or show just about every night of the week, yet I don't have to go into debt to pay my mortgage, as I would back up North. And having come from a region where saying "hello" to strangers will get you branded as slightly loony, I love the warm greeting I receive wherever I go. It's impossible to feel like too much of a stranger in Georgia.

I'm also awed by the contrasts here: the rugged mountains to the north and the pristine beaches to the southeast; the massive skyscrapers shadowing the traditional white-columned architecture; the mega-malls and the old-fashioned country stores. There's something magical about the constant juxtaposition of classic and modern, and surprisingly, the two never seem to get in each other's way here.

I know that I'm far from being the only Yank to succumb to Georgia's charms. Ask just about anyone in the Atlanta area where they're from, and their answer will likely be anywhere *but* Georgia. Just look at the state's soaring population numbers, and you can see how massive the migration has become.

The obvious question is, why does everyone stick around? Some cite the mild climate, which lets them wear short sleeves in the middle of January but still enjoy the occasional white Christmas. Others mention the low cost of living, which allows even Georgians with moderate incomes to afford houses with Jacuzzi bathtubs and big backyards (a fact that's been pulling northerners southward like a magnet). Yet others say it's the economic opportunities that make Georgia the fourth fastest-growing state in the nation.

There is undeniably something magnetic about this state. It goes far beyond the local attractions—the Braves, Coca-Cola, CNN and Stone Mountain—though they certainly are draws. Maybe it's that Georgia has managed to somehow remain entirely faithful to its history and traditions while fully embracing modernity. Even as the cities here expand outward and businesses boom, there always seems to be time to sit back and enjoy a quieter pace of life. I think I'll stick around for a while.

–Stephanie

WHY GEORGIA'S ON EVERYBODY'S MIND

Other arms reach out to me
Other eyes smile tenderly
Still in peaceful dreams I see
The road leads back to you.

"Georgia on My Mind"
–Stuart Gorrell

Sandwiched in the middle of South Carolina, Tennessee, Alabama and Florida, Georgia is easy to overlook. After all, it doesn't have the slick tourist appeal of Florida or the folksy country charm of Tennessee. In fact, the state at first glance seems to blend right in with the southern scenery—lots of green space with a few mountains and beaches thrown in for texture. Look more closely, though, and you will begin to understand what drew wave after wave of European immigrants to Georgia hundreds of years ago and what today continues to drive would-be transplants here in droves.

What might initially appear to be nondescript topography is actually a rich and varied landscape. At every corner of the state is some natural feature that warrants a second glance. To the north, the rugged Blue Ridge Mountains taper off, gradually giving way to the rolling green Piedmont region in the center, where many of the state's major cities and industries are clustered. The Coastal Plain stretches green and fertile across the bottom portion of the state, and the coastal regions are rich in salt marshlands, freshwater swamps and pristine beaches.

Georgia's history is inextricably woven into its landscape. It's impossible to visit without being awed by the state's powerful sense of its own past. The most obvious example of the almost reverential awe with which locals regard their history is the monumental Civil War rock carving in the center of Stone Mountain Park. But there are also more subtle clues: meticulously restored forts and covered bridges, antebellum white-columned homes and battle memorials.

Although many Georgians would rather forget some moments—slavery, the Trail of Tears and Sherman's March— there were also great triumphs throughout Georgia's history. The state was the birthplace of Martin Luther King Jr., after all, and thanks to him, it is the heart of the civil rights movement. Georgia has long been a center for music and culture as well. Ray Charles, Otis Redding, R.E.M. and Trisha Yearwood all got their starts here. And the state is the mecca of southern sports—the place where Hank Aaron broke Babe Ruth's home-run record and Bobby Jones became a golf legend.

Georgia is all about the merging of old and new. Within the space of a few steps, you can slather butter on a homemade bis-cuit and hear, "Y'all come back now!" or buy a Rolex watch and see a world-class theater production. It's a place where traditions are treasured, yet innovation is celebrated.

For all the reasons that make this state so special, these days it seems Georgia is on just about everybody's mind.

OFFICIALLY GEORGIA

In Honor of the King

When it comes to making history, Georgia is among the nation's cornerstones. As the last of 13 original British colonies to form, the original Province of Georgia was named in honor of King George II of England in 1733. On January 2, 1788, Georgia became the fourth state to enter the Union.

Nicknames

Georgia has not one, but several nicknames. It's likely most commonly known as the "Peach State" because of what many believe to be the superior quality of peaches produced there. Georgia picked up two more monikers referring to its economic leadership: "Empire State of the South" and "Yankee-land of the South."

At some point in Georgia's history, buzzards were protected by law, hence the acquired nickname "Buzzard State." And then, of course, there's "Goober State," which is not an insult to the state's residents, but is instead a reference to Georgia's abundant peanut crop. The term "Cracker State" is actually unflattering, since "cracker" is a derogatory term used to describe a poor white person from the South.

State Flag

Although the naming of the state was fairly straightforward, the road to adopting an official flag encountered a few twists and turns. Part of the reason for this was the sentiment of the Georgians at the time who favored secession, and the several unofficial flag designs to fly over the state were called Secession Flags.

The first flag appeared in Savannah on November 8, 1860. It boldly proclaimed "Our Motto, Southern States, Equality of the States, Don't Tread on Me." A flag design commonly used by states wanting to secede had a blue background and a single white star in its center, or a white background and a single red star in its center, and for a time such a flag flew over the state. After Georgia became the fifth state to secede from the Union, it operated under a number of national flags until October 17, 1879, when a first, official Georgia flag was adopted. Influenced somewhat by the first national flag flown by the seceded states, this Georgia flag had one vertical blue bar on the left side, and three horizontal bars—red, white and red—covered the remaining flag. In 1902, as part of the reorganization of state militia laws, the state's coat of arms was added to the flag, centered on the vertical blue bar portion. In 1914, the date on the state seal was changed, and this necessitated a similar date change to the flag. In the 1920s, the seal replaced the coat of arms, though sources are unclear as to why this came about.

In 1955, another design was proposed. This one combined the state seal, but the remaining portion incorporated the earlier

Confederate battle flag, with its red background and large blue "X" sporting 13 evenly spaced white stars. It was officially adopted in 1956.

But the Georgia flag wasn't anywhere near its final incarnation. At the turn of the 21st century, it became such a contentious issue that some believe the flag actually changed the course of a gubernatorial election. Some Georgians saw the Confederate battle emblem on the flag as a symbol of racism. Others felt that it was a proud emblem of Georgia's history. Then Governor Roy Barnes, trying to find a compromise, created a hybrid containing smaller emblems of previous Georgia flags—including the Confederate battle flag—in a small banner entitled "Georgia's History," but the main focus of that flag was the state seal surrounded by the 13 stars representing the original 13 colonies. Southern heritage groups who wanted to return to the 1956 flag were not appeased.

In 2002, Sonny Perdue challenged Roy Barnes for the governor's seat and won. His battle cry during the election was that the people of Georgia should decide on their own flag. In 2003, the Georgia legislature approved his version of the flag, which had the state seal centered on a square of blue in the upper left corner. A solid banner of red ran across the entire bottom of the flag with two smaller bars above it, one white and the other red. A referendum vote was taken on March 2, 2004, to choose between the 2003 rendition and the 2001 version of the flag, and the 2003 design won by a 3–1 margin. Although the vote seemed to seal the flag's fate, the debate was far from over for some southern heritage groups. Long after the referendum, signs proclaiming, "Sonny lied," popped up on front lawns across the state.

State Motto, State Seal

Although Georgia boasts two state mottoes, they weren't
adopted solely for that purpose. Instead, what are commonly
referred to as Georgia's state mottoes are the inscriptions on
either side of the state seal: "Agriculture and Commerce;
Wisdom, Justice and Moderation." Because the front of the state
seal, bearing "Wisdom, Justice and Moderation," is most fre-
quently used in an official capacity, this phrase is the more recognized of the two. The state seal was officially adopted in
1799, which was the original date it bore, but that was changed
on August 17, 1914. That's when the state legislature decided to
replace the date with 1776, which was the year of the
Declaration of Independence.

State Creed

Likely every school-aged youngster has this memorized by now,
but just in case, the Georgia state creed is below in its entirety.
The creed was adopted in 1939.

Accepting, as I do, the principles upon which Georgia was
founded, not for self but others;—its Democratic form of
Government, based on "Wisdom, Justice and
Moderation";—its natural resources;—its Educational,
Social and Religious advantages, making it a most desirable
place to live—I will strive to be a pure upright Citizen,
rejecting the evils—loving and emulating the good.

I further believe it is my duty to defend it against all ene-
mies, to honor and obey its laws, to apply the Golden Rule
in all my dealings with my fellow Citizens.

I feel a sense of pride in the history and heroic deeds accom-
plished by my forebears, and shall endeavor to so live that
my State will be proud of me for doing my bit to make my
State a better Commonwealth for future generations.

Other State Symbols and Emblems

☞ Aside from the state seal, which was adopted in 1814, Georgia's floral emblem is its oldest symbol. In 1816 the Cherokee rose (*Rosa laevigata*) was named the state's official flower.

☞ Georgians are mighty fine bird-lovin' folks. Schoolchildren had already chosen the brown thrasher (*Toxostoma rufum*) as the state bird in 1928, but it wasn't made official until April 6, 1935, with a proclamation by Governor Eugene Talmadge. In 1970, the Garden Clubs of Georgia petitioned the General Assembly to name the bobwhite quail as Georgia's official game bird. It was approved on March 20 of that year.

- It was mostly due to the efforts of the National Society of the Daughters of the American Revolution, who pointed out that the live oak was native to Georgia, that it was named the official state tree. It received that distinction in 1937.

- "Our Georgia," by James Burch, was named Georgia's state waltz in 1951.

- In 1970, the state legislature named the largemouth bass as Georgia's official state fish.

- The Dorothy Alexander Concert Group, a ballet named for its founder in 1929, was the precursor to the Atlanta Ballet. In 1973 it was honored with the distinction of being the state's official ballet.

- Honey is a $70 million a year industry in Georgia, and to honor the hardworking creatures that create the delicious treat, the honeybee (*Apis mellifera*) was named the state's official insect in 1975.

- In 1976, the shark tooth was named the state's official fossil, and quartz was named its official gem.

- The reddish-brown, opaque-looking silicate mineral called staurolite earned the title of Georgia's official state mineral in 1976.

- It was written in 1930 by Stuart Gorrell and Hoagy Carmichael, but "Georgia on My Mind" didn't become the official state song until 1979, and it didn't become a hit until Georgia native Ray Charles made it his own. Since then, the slogan has been emblazoned on everything from license plates to lottery tickets.

- Also in 1979, the azalea (*Rhododendron spp.*) earned the title of official state wildflower.

- The Georgia Museum of Art, which is located at the University of Georgia in Athens, first opened its doors in the basement of a campus library in 1948. Today, the museum has grown to include 8000 items in its permanent collection, and in 1982 it was recognized as the state's official art museum.

- The Atlas of Georgia, complete with transparencies, was named the official state atlas in 1985.

- The right whale (*Eubalaena*), which can grow to a length of 60 feet and weigh upwards of 100 tons, was named Georgia's official marine mammal in 1985.

- In 1987, the knobbed whelk earned the title of state seashell.

- The distinctive black and gold tiger swallowtail (*Papilio glaucus*) was named Georgia's official state butterfly in 1988.

- The gopher tortoise (*Gopherus polyphemus*) earned the title of official state reptile in 1989.

- "The Reach of Song" was named the state's official historic drama in 1990. That was the same year the Vidalia sweet onion was named the official state vegetable.

- Georgia has an official 'possum. Pogo 'Possum, a cartoon character created in 1943 by Walt Kelly, was officially designated as such in 1992. The comic strip first ran in the *New York Star* when it launched on October 4, 1948, but was rapidly syndicated and appeared in daily newspapers across the country from 1949 to 1975. The main star of the show was, of course, Pogo the 'Possum. Although Kelly was not a native of Georgia, his creation was made the official state 'possum because the characters in the strip (some have estimated there were more than 300) were modeled after animals found in the Okefenokee Swamp, located along the Georgia-Florida border.

☛ The North Georgia Folk Festival, which first began entertaining music lovers in 1984, was named the state's official folk festival in 1992. That same year the Springer Opera House in Columbus was named the official state theater.

☛ Created by Valdosta State College, the Jekyll Island Musical Theatre Festival earned the designation of state musical theater in 1993.

☛ With a nickname like the Peach State, it makes good sense that the perfect, plump produce was named Georgia's official fruit in 1995.

☛ With a heel, a toe and a do-si-do, the square dance was named Georgia's official folk dance in 1996.

☞ Also in 1996, the Central of Georgia Railroad Shops Complex in Savannah was named the state's official railroad museum.

☞ It may be accented with a thick drawl at times, but English has been the official state language in Georgia since 1996.

☞ If you're interested in "shooting the bull" while stirring a steaming pot of chili, the Hawkinsville Civitan Club's "Shoot the Bull" barbecue championship is the place for you. In 1997, the state legislature named the event the state's official beef barbecue championship cook-off.

☞ James Earl (Jimmy) Carter Jr. was the only Georgia-born president of the United States. Plains High School, where he attended, was honored with the title of official state school in 1997.

☞ The Slosheye Trail Big Pig Jig in Vienna has been feeding and entertaining folks since 1982, and in 1997, it was named the state's official pork barbecue championship cook-off.

☞ The Georgia Tartan, with its beautiful deep greens and brilliant reds, was first introduced to the public in 1982, but wasn't designated the state's official tartan until 1997.

☞ In 2000, the Southeastern Railway Museum in Duluth was named the state's official transportation history museum.

☞ Bet if you asked just about anyone what they thought the state's official prepared food was, they'd say grits—and they'd be right, too. It was so named in 2002.

☞ The Mighty Eighth Air Force Heritage Museum was named the state's official Center for Character Education in 2003.

☞ The Funk Heritage Center at Reinhardt College in Waleska was named Georgia's official Frontier and Southeastern Indian Interpretive Center in 2003.

☞ The green tree frog (*Hyla cinerea*), common to the wilds of Georgia, is considered by many to be one of the most beautiful species of its kind on the continent. In fact, it's such a fine specimen that it was used as the basis for the Kermit the Frog character. It was honored in 2005 with the distinction of being the state's official amphibian.

CREATING A STATE

On a Mission

Ten thousand years ago, Native American tribes inhabited the land that is now Georgia. The Creek and Cherokee Natives once made up the majority of Georgia's population. But as was the case in other areas of the country, European explorers came in and took possession of the land—usually for a bargain price. The first to arrive in Georgia was Spanish explorer Hernando de Soto, who came in search of gold. The gold was here, but de Soto never found it.

Exploration turned into something more permanent when Spanish sailor and explorer Pedro Menendez de Aviles (who had successfully established Franciscan missions near St. Augustine, Florida) expanded into Georgia. The goal of the missions was purportedly to save the Native Americans' souls, but the explorers were actually on the hunt for cheap labor. They thought that by "converting" the Guale and Timucuan Natives into loyal Spanish subjects, they could force them into working for the colony. The first mission, San Pedro de Mocama, was established in what is now Cumberland Island, a barrier island along the Georgia coast. The missions continued to preach until around 1684, when the English began jostling for control of the area and the Spanish missionaries were forced to pack up their Bibles and move on.

By George-ia!

When the British set their sights on Georgia, they had an ulterior motive. They controlled South Carolina, but the Spanish ran Florida, and the two nations weren't exactly best friends. The British thought it would be a good idea to set up a sort of buffer zone in between the two states. A Parliament member named James Edward Oglethorpe spearheaded the move and formed a corporation that eventually became known as the Georgia Trustees. Oglethorpe also had another plan for the region: he wanted it to become a place of refuge for debtors who were locked up in British prisons. He figured the British government would be better served having the debtors working for the benefit of the realm, rather than rotting away in jail.

In 1732, King George II finally gave his blessing, and as a way of saying thanks, the new settlement was given his name—Georgia. Oglethorpe and his group of 114 settlers landed in Savannah on February 12, 1733. There to welcome them was Chief Tomochichi of the local Yamacraw Natives.

The rules for the new settlers were strict: they had to promise to work for the colony for three years and plant mulberry trees in which to breed silkworms. Slavery was forbidden, as was the importing of rum, which Oglethorpe and the trustees feared would make the colonists lazy. But human nature being what it is, these prohibitions didn't last long. When things didn't work out as well as they had planned in the new colony, the trustees eventually lost interest. They returned their charter to George II in 1752 and Georgia came under new management.

When the colony of Georgia was first created in 1732, its motto was "Non sibi sed aliis," which is Latin for, "Not for oneself but for others." The goal was for a version of utopian society, where every one of the colonists would have an equal share of the land and would work together to build the new colony.

The Capital Shuffle

Georgia's capital changed a dizzying number of times throughout its history. See if you can keep up with these moves:

1777–78	Savannah
1779–80	Augusta
1780–81	Heard's Fort
1781–82	Augusta
1782	Savannah
1783	Augusta
1784	Savannah
1784	Augusta
1785	Savannah
1786–96	Augusta
1796–1806	Louisville
1807–64	Milledgeville
1864–65	Macon

(special sessions of Georgia's assembly were held here while Union forces controlled Milledgeville)

1865–68	Milledgeville
1868–today	Atlanta

FOUNDING FATHERS

James Edward Oglethorpe (1696–1785)

Without James Edward Oglethorpe, Georgia could never have existed. Born in London, England, in 1696, Oglethorpe came from strong military and political roots. His father was an officer in the army and a member of the British House of Commons. Oglethorpe dropped out of school at an early age to enroll in a military academy in France. He eventually returned to London, and in 1722, he was elected to Parliament, taking over his father's seat in the House of Commons.

When Oglethorpe saw his good friend Robert Castell get thrown in prison for debts and ultimately die there of smallpox, he went on a crusade to reform England's prisons. He set up the Georgia colony as a refuge for debtors, though few of them actually made it there. As the Georgia colony's first leader, Oglethorpe was uncharacteristically tolerant for the time. He prohibited slavery and allowed Jews and other persecuted religious groups to settle in the region. But in 1743, trouble erupted and Oglethorpe was forced to return to England to face allegations of misconduct brought against him by one of his subordinates. Although the charges were dropped, Oglethorpe never returned to the colony he had founded. He died in his native land on June 30, 1785.

Sir James Wright

The third and most popular of Georgia's royal governors, Sir James Wright (his predecessors were John Reynolds and Henry Ellis) took office in 1760 and quickly amassed a huge fortune. He owned 11 plantations extending over 25,000 acres and had more than 500 slaves—not exactly a proud feat when recalled today, but slavery was allowed in Georgia after 1750. Wright also expanded Georgia's borders with the Treaty of Augusta in 1763.

Once the Revolution got started in 1776, Georgia rebels arrested Wright, but he managed to escape and boarded a ship bound home to England. He came back to Georgia in 1779 because the locals were fighting to take back Savannah from the Brits. Wright served in the States for three more years until the British finally hightailed it out of Savannah for good on July 11, 1782.

DID YOU KNOW?

In 1774, Georgia was the only state that didn't send a representative to the First Continental Congress in Philadelphia. However, three Georgia congressional delegates did make it to Philadelphia on August 2, 1776, to sign the Declaration of Independence.

Independence-Minded Georgians

Georgia had three signers of the Declaration of Independence: Button Gwinnett, Lyman Hall and George Walton. The English-born Gwinnett (1735–77) was a member of Georgia's colonial legislature. He was killed in a duel with his political rival, Lachlan McIntosh in 1777. Hall (1724–90) was a doctor who was born in Connecticut. He was part of Georgia's revolutionary movement and served as a representative to the Continental Congress. Walton (1750–1804) had one of the most successful law practices in the colony. He served as a delegate to the Continental Congress in 1776.

The Yazoo Land Fraud

After the Revolution, Georgia had vast areas of unprotected land, called "Yazoo lands," which today are Alabama and Mississippi. Using bribery and intimidation, four companies— the Georgia Company, the Georgia-Mississippi Company, the Upper Mississippi Company and the Tennessee Company— managed to persuade the Georgia legislature to pass a bill called the Yazoo Act. It allowed the companies to purchase 35 million acres of land for the ridiculously low price (even back then) of $500,000 in 1795 dollars. Public opposition was so fierce that many of the politicians involved in the fraud were ousted from office. In a charge led by U.S. Senator James Jackson, the Act was repealed on February 18, 1795.

This Date in Georgia History

- April 21, 1732—King George II signed Georgia's charter, paving the way for a settlement of British colonists.

- 1758—Georgia's parish system of government was established. By 1777 it was replaced by the county system, which still exists today.

- 1763—The Georgia colony's first newspaper, the *Georgia Gazette*, launched.

- June 1777—Georgia adopted its first state constitution.

- 1782—The British evacuated Savannah, ending royal rule in Georgia.

- January 2, 1788—Georgia ratified the United States Constitution, becoming the fourth state to do so.

- 1825—George M. Troup defeated Matthew Talbot to be re-elected governor in the state's first popular gubernatorial election.

- 1828—Gold was discovered in the north Georgia mountains, and the Georgia Gold Rush was underway.

- 1833—President Andrew Jackson evicted Cherokee tribes from the gold-rich areas of North Georgia. His troops pulled the Cherokee from their homes and forced them to march 1000 miles in what became known as the Trail of Tears.

- 1845—The city of Atlanta got its name.

- January 19, 1861—Georgia became the fifth state to secede from the Union, leading to the Civil War.

- September 2, 1864—Atlanta surrendered to General William Tecumseh Sherman.

- November 1866—Slavery was abolished, and slaves were freed in Georgia.

- July 1870—Georgia was readmitted to the Union.

MILITARY SKIRMISHES

The Battle of Bloody Marsh

From the time they arrived in the South, British colonists were on shaky ground with their Spanish neighbors. In July 1742, the situation exploded when a fleet of 50 Spanish ships attacked James Edward Oglethorpe's men on St. Simons Island. The Spanish forces, led by Don Manuel de Montiano, the governor of St. Augustine, Florida, numbered about 5000 men. Oglethorpe had just 1000 soldiers, most of them British and Native American. Even though they were vastly outnumbered, Oglethorpe's troops fought back valiantly and eventually defeated the Spanish.

DID YOU KNOW?

Despite its gory name, the Battle of Bloody Marsh had relatively few casualties. Only about 50 men were killed.

Civil War Moments

The Civil War was such an integral part of Georgia's history that to some people, it still lives on today (and to many, the South actually won). Here are just a few of the decisive moments that shaped the Civil War:

☞ April 10, 1862—Union forces under the direction of General Quincy A. Gilmore pounded Fort Pulaski with 5000 shells at the mouth of the Savannah River. Although the fort was built to be impenetrable, the shelling was so intense over a 36-hour period that Confederate commander Colonel Charles Olmstead had no choice but to surrender on the afternoon of April 11. The loss of Fort Pulaski blocked off a critical route for the Confederate Army.

☛ June 11, 1863—The all-black Union regiment, the 54th Massachusetts (featured in the movie *Glory*), looted the virtually undefended town of Darien and burned just about every structure to the ground.

☛ September 18–20, 1863—Confederate forces under the direction of General Braxton Bragg pushed General William S. Rosecrans and his Union troops back to Chattanooga. It was one of the bloodiest battles in the Civil War, with 16,000 Union soldiers and more than 18,000 Confederate soldiers killed.

☛ May 1864—General William Tecumseh Sherman advanced toward Atlanta with three armies made up of more than 100,000 men.

☛ June 27, 1864—Confederate soldiers were able to hold back Sherman's push toward Atlanta in the Battle of Kennesaw Mountain. The Union troops lost about 3000 men, and Confederate losses numbered less than 1000.

☛ September 1, 1864—Despite the small setback at Kennesaw Mountain, Sherman's troops took over Atlanta, dealing a staggering blow to the Confederate Army, and then burned the city to the ground.

Horrors of Andersonville Prison

It was open for barely more than a year (from February 1864 to April 1865), yet Andersonville Prison became known as one of the most notoriously brutal POW camps of the Civil War. Although it was only built large enough to house 10,000 soldiers, Andersonville held more than 33,000 Union soldiers at one time. Nearly 13,000 died from disease, malnutrition and exposure. The place was so vile that following the war, its commandant was hanged.

The Great Locomotive Chase

You've heard of car thieves, but how about train thieves? On April 12, 1862, James J. Andrews and his band of Union soldiers disguised themselves as civilians and stole the General locomotive at Big Shanty (now Kennesaw) while the train's crew was eating breakfast at the nearby Lacy Hotel. Confederate Conductor William Fuller saw the train pulling out of the station and gave chase in a handcar. He finally caught up with the Union general and his men just before they reached Chattanooga, Tennessee. Andrews was tried as a spy and hanged, along with seven of his men. Several of the other men escaped. The Union soldiers involved in the chase were later awarded the very first Medals of Honor.

March to the Sea

After capturing Atlanta and burning down every major structure in the city, General Sherman began his March to the Sea in November 1864. He captured Savannah in December, before moving into South Carolina. Along his route, Sherman destroyed everything in his path, including railroads, factories and even homes—anything that Confederate soldiers might have used to their advantage.

On December 21, 1864, Sherman sent this famous message to President Lincoln: "I beg to present you, as a Christmas Gift, the City of Savannah, with 150 heavy guns and plenty of ammunition, and also about 25,000 bales of cotton."

A Terrible Toll

Out of the estimated 125,000 Georgians who fought on the side of the Confederacy, some 25,000 lost their lives. The census of 1870 listed 100,000 fewer men between the ages of 20 and 29 than had the census the year before.

DID YOU KNOW?

You might have thought that military battles in Georgia ended with the Civil War, but that isn't quite true. During World War II—on the evening of April 8, 1942, to be exact—the German submarine U-123 torpedoed and sank two American tankers—the *SS Oklahoma* and the *Esso Baton Rouge*—just off the coast of St. Simons Island.

The Civil Rights Movement

Atlanta became the center of the civil rights movement, driven by the conviction and perseverance of these leaders:

☛ W.E.B. DuBois—In the early 1900s, this Atlanta University sociologist pushed for equal political and social rights for African Americans. He was one of the founding fathers of the National Association for the Advancement of Colored People (NAACP).

☛ Martin Luther King Jr.—The undisputed leader of the civil rights movement, and Atlanta's favorite son, Martin Luther King Jr. was born in 1929. He graduated from Atlanta's Morehouse College, received his PhD from Boston University and was ordained a minister in 1947. In 1955, after Rosa Parks was arrested for refusing to move to the back of the bus, King led the famous Montgomery, Alabama,

bus boycott. In 1957, he was elected president of the
Southern Christian Leadership Conference. His most famous
moment came on August 23, 1963, when he delivered his
"I Have a Dream" speech at the Lincoln Memorial in
Washington, DC.

On the night of April 4, 1968, as he stood on the balcony of
the Lorraine Motel in Memphis, Tennessee, King was
assassinated by James Earl Ray. Even after his death, King's
memory continued to fuel the civil rights movement until his
dream was realized and African Americans were granted
equal rights.

☛ Andrew Young—Young worked alongside Martin Luther
King Jr. in the Southern Christian Leadership Conference
and was by his side when King was assassinated. After King's
death, Young served as congressman, ambassador to the
United Nations and two-term Atlanta mayor. He was instrumental in promoting African American voter registration
programs and helped former president Jimmy Carter further
the cause of human rights throughout the world.

☛ Hosea Williams—A former aide to Martin Luther King Jr., Williams was a leader in the Southern Christian Leadership Conference and a major force in the civil rights movement. On March 7, 1965, he and John Lewis led the Selma, Alabama, protest march, which became known as "Bloody Sunday," after police attacked the nonviolent protesters with clubs and tear gas. In 1971, Williams founded the organization, Hosea Feed the Hungry and Homeless, which has so far distributed more than $3 billion in food, clothing and other necessities to Georgia's homeless people.

☛ W.W. Law—The president of the Savannah NAACP chapter was known as "Mr. Civil Rights" for his tireless crusade against segregation. In 1962, he brought a suit against the Savannah-Chatham County public schools, and he led boycotts against stores that wouldn't serve African Americans. His efforts led to desegregation in Savannah by 1963, several months before federal laws went into effect.

WEATHERING THE WEATHER

Mild Winters, Sultry Summers

Moderate winter temperatures and hot, moist summers describe much of Georgia's climate. Generally speaking, climate and precipitation rates vary slightly within the state's three regions:

☛ The mountainous area to the north, which includes the Blue Ridge, Ridge and Valley, and Appalachian Plateau, typically experiences more precipitation in the spring and summer months and is drier in fall and winter—between October 1928 and October 1963, as little as 0.01 inches of rain fell during some months. Of course, there's always the exception to every rule. On September 9, 1975, 10 inches of rain fell in Dalton within a 24-hour period. This area of the state also receives the greatest amount of snowfall in any given year. In the great blizzard of 1993, as much as two feet of the white powder covered the area. Elevation differences throughout the region also contribute to the wide variety of average temperatures experienced there.

☛ Georgia's Piedmont Plateau, running from the foothills of the Appalachians to the Coastal Plain, takes up roughly one-third of the state and ranges in elevation from 500 to 1500 feet above sea level. With average annual temperatures of about 74°F, roughly 40-plus inches of precipitation each year and soil primed for agriculture, it's no wonder this area is known for its production of cotton, peaches and other crops.

☛ The southern three-fifths of Georgia is the Coastal Plain region. Elevation here ranges from sea level to 600 feet, and temperatures are typically warm, with the average high around 77°F and the average low around 54°F. That doesn't mean the area doesn't have its share of extremes. During summer, temperatures in some coastal locations can soar to 100°F or higher. And other areas, such as Albany, can experience as many as 97 days a year with temperatures in excess of 90°F. Folks living in this region can expect about 121 rainy days a year and about 45 inches of precipitation, on average.

Average Temperature

As a rule, monthly temperatures in Georgia range from an average high of 92.2°F to an average low of 32.6°F.

High Temperature

On July 24, 1953, Louisville recorded Georgia's highest temperature to date, at a whopping 112°F.

Low Temperature

The mercury dipped to –17°F on January 27, 1940, at the Civilian Conservation Corps Camp in North Georgia and was the state's lowest recorded temperature.

Average Rainfall

Taking all the elevation factors and proximity to mountains and ocean into consideration, Georgia usually receives between 40 and 50 inches of rain each year. Here's what the precipitation looked like in some regions over the years. *(Source: Georgia State Climate Office)*

City	One Day Max	Date	Annual Mean
Americus	21.10 inches	July 6, 1994	49.04 inches
Athens	9.93 inches	June 4, 1967	49.56 inches
Savannah	8.47 inches	Sept. 5, 1950	49.56 inches
Rome	6.67 inches	Oct. 26, 1997	54.83 inches
Macon	2.29 inches	Nov. 27, 1948	44.99 inches

WILD WEATHER

Holy Tornado!

Georgia experiences about six tornados a year. Thankfully, most of these are rated F0 or F1—storms with winds only strong enough to break off tree branches and cause moderate damage to roofs and signs. However, 37 percent of Georgia's tornados are rated F2 and higher and are quite capable of causing extensive damage, injury and death. Here are a few tornado tidbits:

- Forty-eight percent of the tornados to hit Georgia between 1950 and 1995 occurred during the spring.

- Georgia experiences more tornados in April than in any other month of the year.

- September has fewer tornados than any other month of the year.

☛ Eighty Georgians have died and another 2000 have been injured in tornados over the last 40 years.

☛ The state's most deadly tornado hit Gainesville on April 6, 1932, and 203 people died.

☛ Georgia was one of 13 states affected by the worst tornado outbreak in U.S. history. On April 3 and 4, 1974, 148 separate twisters were confirmed as touching down. Seven of them landed in Georgia, causing 17 deaths, 104 injuries and about $15 million in property damage.

Quaking Underfoot

Although not an overly common occurrence, Georgia has had the occasional earthquake. The ripple effects from three earthquakes in the range of 7.2–8.1 magnitude that hit New Madrid, Missouri, in late 1811 and early 1812 were also felt by Georgians. Although they occurred two states to the northwest, the earthquakes that hit the Mississippi River Valley near New Madrid are considered by the U.S. Geological Survey as "some of the largest in the United States since its settlement by Europeans," far outweighing the strength of the great San Francisco earthquake of 1906 and the Alaska earthquake of 1964. Savannah residents felt the effects of four separate shockwaves on December 16 and 17, 1811. Here are a few other earth-shattering moments to remember:

☛ In 1886, a great earthquake hit Charleston, South Carolina, sending shock waves as far away as Savannah, which toppled chimneys, cracked walls and even frightened one woman to death. Augusta was the hardest hit area in Georgia, with 1000 chimneys and numerous buildings damaged.

☛ That same earthquake caused a crack near the middle of a 134-foot-tall lighthouse at the Tybee Island Light Station. Considering that the station's walls are six feet thick, that was some tremor.

- Windows rattled in Milledgeville on June 17, 1872, when an earthquake measuring 5 on the Modified Mercalli Intensity Scale rumbled the region.

- A widespread area of Georgia, from Atlanta and Macon to Gainesville and Augusta, felt the earth move when an earthquake rocked the South Carolina border on November 1, 1875.

- More tremors rumbled west of Dalton and around La Fayette on October 18, 1902.

- Communities from Savannah to Augusta and Charleston to Columbia experienced earthquakes of varying magnitudes on January 23, 1903. The center of this geological event was Tybee Island and covered an area of about 10,000 square miles.

- Thirty miles southeast of Atlanta was the center of a minor earthquake on March 5, 1916.

- The ground rumbled for about 400 square miles surrounding Haddock when a minor earthquake hit on March 12, 1964.

Emergency Declarations

In the last 30 years, Georgia has been under a state of emergency six times. Most recently, and still active, is the Hurricane Katrina Evacuation of September 2005. Other emergency declarations included:

- Hurricane Floyd in September 1999

- A winter storm with heavy snowfall in March 1993

- Spring storms and tornados in May 1984

- Drought in July 1977

- Tornados in March 1975

WHERE'S GEORGIA AT?

Know Your Neighbors

Georgia is surrounded by Tennessee and North Carolina to the north, South Carolina and the Atlantic Ocean to the east, Florida to the south, and Alabama to the west.

Size Matters
Of the 50 states, Georgia ranks 24th largest, covering 59,441 square miles.

Georgia's Center Point

The geographic center of Georgia is in Twiggs County, 18 miles southeast of Macon.

Surf and Turf
With 1522 square miles of the wet stuff, just less than three percent of Georgia consists of water. The remaining 57,919 square miles are all dry land.

Coastland

Georgia has about 100 miles of coastline along the Atlantic Ocean.

Lying Low
Sea level, where Georgia meets the Atlantic Ocean, is the lowest point of elevation in the state.

Islands, Islands, Everywhere
Assorted islands dot Georgia's coastline, as with the majority of the American eastern seaboard. These barrier islands, which are considerably younger than the mainland, first emerged sometime in the last 30,000 to 5000 years. They are largely shaped

by a number of environmental factors, especially by the tide. And because of Georgia's western location, those tides are far more powerful than anywhere else on the eastern seaboard, rising between six- and eight-feet high.

DID YOU KNOW?

Brasstown Bald—also known as Mount Etonah—is the highest point in Georgia. It stands at 4784 feet above sea level.

Middle of the Road

On average, Georgia sits at an elevation of 600 feet above sea level.

Parks and Forests

Georgia has six state forests occupying 63,294 acres, and 64 state parks covering another 65,066 acres of land.

Raging Rivers

The three main rivers in Georgia are the Chattahoochee River, Savannah River and Suwannee River. The Chattahoochee begins its 436-mile-long journey in the northern portion of the state and flows in a southwestern direction into Alabama. The Savannah River measures about 350 miles in length and pretty much follows the border between Georgia and South Carolina. The Suwannee River measures about 266 miles in length and flows from the southern part of Georgia into Florida.

The Big Splash!

Georgia is home to five major lakes: Clarks Hill Lake, Lake George, Lake Hartwell, Lake Lanier and Lake Seminole.

COUNTY TALES

Countdown

Based on size, here are the 10 largest Georgia counties:

County	Area (square miles)
Ware	906.6
Burke	835.1
Clinch	824.2
Laurens	818.6
Charlton	783.0
Camden	782.5
Emanuel	690.4
Bulloch	688.9
Washington	684.4
Screven	655.7

County Curiosities

There are 159 counties in Georgia. Here's something interesting about a few of them:

☛ War of 1812 hero, Lieutenant Colonel Daniel Appling, was honored in the naming of Appling County.

☛ Ben Hill County was formed by a constitutional amendment on July 31, 1906. It is one of 25 Georgian counties that retained its original boundaries.

☛ Bulloch County calls itself "one of Georgia's fastest growing and progressive counties." Its motto is "First in Safety and Services."

- Not to be outdone, Cherokee County makes a similar claim to being one of the state's fastest growing counties. Its motto is "Where Metro Meets the Mountains."

- More than one-third, or 14,387, of Colquitt County's 42,053 residents live in the city of Moultrie, the county seat.

- Cordele is the county seat of Crisp County. The city calls itself the "Watermelon Capital of the World."

- Early County wasn't part of the original Colony of Georgia. Before either the Confederate States of America or United States flag flew overhead, Spain, France and England all had their turn laying claim to the area.

- Habersham County is home to the famed Tallulah Falls. Two daring attempts have been made to traverse the 1200-foot-wide falls, which plunge 1000 feet to the river below, via tightrope. J.A. St. John, who went by the name of Professor Leon, made the first attempt in 1886, and Karl Wallenda of the famous circus family "The Great Wallendas" attempted the feat in 1970. Both were successful.

- Gilmer County calls itself Georgia's "apple capital." It harvests about 600,000 bushels of the fruit each year.

☛ Harts County is named after the Revolutionary War heroine Nancy Harts—it's the only county in the state to be named after a woman.

☛ Roughly 14 percent of Lumpkin County is farmland.

☛ Tiff County claims to be home to the "largest southern magnolia in Georgia and among the oldest anywhere."

ANIMAL KINGDOM

Warm-Blooded

Aside from man, there are about 93 different species of mammals found in Georgia. Of this number, several are endangered, extinct, rare, unusual, threatened or extirpated. Here's a breakdown of some of the rarer species:

☞ The gray myotis and Indiana myotis, two species in the *Vespertilionidae* family of bats, are listed as both federally endangered and Georgia endangered. Their range is significantly smaller than the other species of the bat family, and both occupy the northwestern portion of the state, but the gray myotis to a lesser extent. These bats are typically small, measuring between 3.1 and 3.7 inches and are recognized by their mouse-like ears.

☞ The Rafinesque's big-eared bat is seen throughout many of the southern states but is considered rare in Georgia. The bat has the unique habit of twisting and folding its ears down its back when resting.

☞ The nocturnal nine-banded armadillo isn't native to Georgia. The species is believed to have slipped into the state after it was introduced into Florida sometime in the late 1800s.

☞ Typically occupying the southernmost portion of the state, the round-tail muskrat is one of Georgia's threatened species.

☞ The black rat, Norway rat, house mouse, mouse beaver, wild pig and fallow deer were all introduced into Georgia.

☞ At an adult length of up to 57 feet, the black right whale is one of the state's largest mammals. But big doesn't always mean indestructible. This water lover is on both the federal and Georgia endangered lists.

☞ The red and gray wolves have become locally extinct in Georgia and are listed as federally endangered species.

☞ The mountain lion and manatee are on both the federal and Georgia endangered lists.

☞ The bison has become extinct in Georgia.

DID YOU KNOW?

Besides Punxsutawney Phil, our country boasts another weather-prognosticating rodent. Georgia has its own furry forecaster, General Beau Lee, PhD. Every Groundhog Day, he emerges from his home at the Yellow River Game Ranch in Lilburn. If he doesn't see his shadow, Georgians can look forward to an early spring. If he does, there'll be six more weeks of winter weather to endure.

Water Lovers

Georgia is home to a long list of salamanders, tree frogs and other amphibians. Among those found in the state are the flatwoods salamander, one-toed amphiuma, hellbender, green salamander, Pigeon Mountain salamander and the striped newt. The only threatened amphibian in the state is the Georgia blind salamander. Reptiles also do quite well in Georgia. Two of the state's 16 lizard species, the mediterranean gecko and the brown anole, were introduced to the state. Besides the lizards, 40 different snake varieties live and thrive in Georgia. Turtles are another matter entirely. Of the 26 varieties that live here, many are either endangered or rare. Here's how the turtle population breaks down:

☞ The loggerhead, green, hawksbill, Atlantic ridley and leatherback turtles are all on both federal and Georgia endangered lists.

☞ The alligator snapping turtle, gopher tortoise and Barbour's map turtle are all on the Georgia threatened species list.

☞ If you see a spotted or bog turtle in Georgia, it's considered an unusual sighting.

☞ The Alabama map and common map turtles are also rare sights in the state.

PLANT LIFE

Leafy Greens

Georgia is home to a vast array of plant life, making the state picturesque in its beauty. But the welfare of many of the native species is of concern either in the state, country or world. Here are some of the species at risk, all of which have been given a G1 ranking. "G1" means there are five or fewer occurrences of the species worldwide, and they are considered critically imperiled.

Alabama leatherflower

Black-spored quillwort

Blomquist leafy liverwort

Bloom quillwort

Brock sweetshrub

Cliffside goldenrod

Cream-flowered tick trefoil

Curtiss' loosestrife

Cuthbert holly

Dixie Mountain breadroot

Downy slender ladies'-tresses

False pimpernel

Floodplain tickseed

Florida ladies'-tresses

Florida torreya

Florida water parsnip

Georgia beaksedge

Georgia rockcress

Grit portulaca

Hairy rattleweed

Hirst's witch grass

Kral's water plantain

Limerock arrow-wood

Liverwort

Mat-forming quillwort

Mock bishop-weed

Narrowleaf naiad

Persistent trillium

Pineland beaksedge

Radford's mint

Roundleaf meadowrue

Rush quillwort

Silver buckthorn

Slender leather-root

Solitary beakrush

Whorled sunflower

POPULATION COUNTS

Georgia Population Through the Years

Census Year	Population
1790	82,548
1800	162,686
1850	906,185
1860	1,057,286
1870	1,184,109
1880	1,541,180
1890	1,837,353
1900	2,216,331
1950	3,444,578
1980	4,589,575
2000	8,186,453

Top Ten

With a total population of 8,186,453 residents, according to the 2000 Census, Georgia is the 10th most populous state in the nation. The 2006 Census estimate suggests the state has seen a population increase of 14.4 percent over the last six years, putting the current population at closer to 9,363,941.

Breaking it Down

Generally speaking, the population of Georgia looks something like this:

☛ 7.6 percent are under the age of five years

☛ 26.0 percent are under 18 years

☛ 9.6 percent are 65 years and older

☛ 50.5 percent are female

☛ 1.1 percent of the population, or about 577,273 people, were born outside the United States

☛ 9.9 percent of those aged five years and older speak a language other than English at home

☛ 24.3 percent of those aged 25 years and older have earned a bachelor's degree, just slightly under the national average of 24.4 percent

☛ Of the population aged five years and older, 1,456,812 people struggle with some type of disability

Ethnic Diversity

The following statistics on the State of Georgia are based on 2006 estimates from the U.S. Census Bureau.

Race	Percentage of Population*
White (non-Hispanic)	58.9
Black	29.9
Hispanic or Latino	7.5
Asian	2.8
Persons with two or more racial backgrounds	1.1
American Indian and Alaska Native	0.3
Native Hawaiian and Other Pacific Islander	0.1

*Note: The "Hispanic or Latino" category can include people of any race, which is why the figures don't add up to 100 percent.

Popular Cities

According to the 2000 Census, Atlanta, with a population of 416,474, is the state's most heavily populated city. Here are the other nine cities that round out the top ten list:

City	Population
Augusta	195,182
Columbus	185,781
Savannah	131,510
Athens	100,266
Macon	97,255
Roswell	79,334
Albany	76,939
Marietta	58,748
Warner Robins	48,804

DID YOU KNOW?

Although North America is a mosaic of various ethnic ancestries, the five most prominent in Georgia are African, American, British, German and Irish.

County by County

Although the largest county in Georgia is Ware—906.6 square miles—its population was recorded at just 34,492 in the 2005 Census. Compare that to the most populous county in the state, Fulton County, whose 815,006 residents live in an area measuring 534.6 square miles, about half the size of Ware County. In descending order, here are the other nine counties that round out the top ten Georgia population list:

County	Population
DeKalb	665,865
Cobb	607,751
Gwinnett	588,448
Clayton	236,517
Chatham	232,048
Richmond	199,775
Muscogee	186,291
Bibb	153,887
Cherokee	141,903

PLACES TO BE IN GEORGIA

Squarely Savannah

Savannah doesn't look like any other place in the country, and that's by design. The city is composed of a series of 24 squares, each of which measures about 200 feet from one end to the other, and sits in the middle of a rectangular ward. James Edward Oglethorpe set up the grid when he arrived here with his group of British settlers in 1733. Yet despite the military precision with which they were laid out, the squares, with their oak trees dripping with Spanish moss, have a stately and almost romantic feel.

Each square is named after an important person or event in the city's history. There's even one named in Oglethorpe's honor, although when it was created in 1742, it was simply known as "Upper New Square."

Here are a few tidbits about some of Savannah's other squares:

☛ Franklin Square was named for Benjamin Franklin, who was Georgia's colony agent to London during Colonial times.

☛ Greene Square is named for General Nathaniel Greene, George Washington's second-in-command during the Revolutionary War.

☛ Johnson Square was the first square in Savannah, created in 1733. It was named after Robert Johnson, who was governor of South Carolina when Georgia became an official colony.

☛ Madison Square was built in 1837 and named in honor of the fourth U.S. president, James Madison. It is home to the

Green Meldrim House, which was once General Sherman's headquarters.

☞ Monterey Square is the location of the famous Mercer House, immortalized in the best-selling book *Midnight in the Garden of Good and Evil*.

☞ Troup Square was named after Georgia Governor Michael Troup. It was one of only two squares named for someone who was still living at the time.

Don't Let the Bed Bugs Bite!

The story behind this famously buggy saying reportedly comes from Savannah. In the old days, colonists stuffed their mattresses with soft Spanish moss, only to wake up scratching furiously from the plant's tiny residents—bed bugs (chiggers). The original phrase in its entirety was, "Goodnight neighbor, sleep tight, and don't let the bed bugs bite!"

DID YOU KNOW?

Chippewa Square was named for a famous battle during the War of 1812, but it's probably best known as the spot where Forrest Gump sat on a bench and mused about life and chocolate in the Academy Award–winning movie of the same name. The bench where Gump's famous "but-tocks" rested has moved to a new home in the Savannah History Museum to protect it from the elements.

Classical Towns

Thousands of miles from the real things are Georgia's own versions of Athens and Rome. Rome even has its own Forum, although unlike the real deal, it's just a large meeting space. Athens, named in honor of Greece's center of learning, is north Georgia's own educational hub and is home to the University of Georgia.

In front of Rome's City Hall stands a bronze statue of Romulus and Remus, the mythological twin brothers who were said to have founded Rome. The statue was a gift from Italian premier Benito Mussolini in 1929. During World War II when Mussolini sided with Hitler, the town removed the statue, only to reinstate it in 1952.

Best Place to Live

This city of 16,000 residents located just a half-hour drive north of Atlanta must be doing something right, because it made number 10 on *Money* magazine's 2007 list of Top 100 Places to Live. The editors cited plenty of green space, affordable housing and "top-notch" schools as the reasons why Suwanee is such a great place to call home.

Capitol City

In the early 1840s, the Western and Atlantic Railroad of the State of Georgia served as a main trade route between Georgia, Tennessee and the northern states. At the end of the railroad line, a small town, aptly named Terminus, grew. In 1843, it was renamed in honor of Martha Lumpkin, daughter of the famous Georgia Governor Wilson Lumpkin. But that moniker didn't last long. By 1845 the city underwent another name change, this time to Atlanta, in honor of the Western and Atlantic Railroad. The city eventually evolved from a railroad hub to the thriving metropolitan area it is today.

Roosevelt's Favorite Retreat

On October 3, 1924, Franklin Delano Roosevelt's doctor advised him to take a vacation to Warm Springs. The warm mineral springs flowing down to the base of Pine Mountain had long been considered to have healing properties. Roosevelt, whose legs had been paralyzed by polio, thought a dip might have curative properties. His first time in the water, Roosevelt exclaimed, "I don't think I will ever get out." He became a regular visitor and set up a treatment center on the site for others stricken with polio. Warm Springs continued to be a favorite retreat when Roosevelt became president, and he even built a six-room cottage there, called The Little White House. It was where he died on April 12, 1945.

WHAT'S IN A NAME?

A Peachtree on Every Corner

With so many streets named Peachtree—at least 32 of them—
it's a wonder that any of Atlanta's tourists can find their way
around! You might think the name's origins have something to
do with the fruit, but there's no evidence that any peach trees
actually existed in the area. Instead, the name is believed to
have come from Standing Peachtree, the Creek Indian village
that once existed along the Chattahoochee River. Some historians have said the name might have been derived from a "pitch
tree" that grew in the old Native American village. Over time,
Peachtree became so popular and prestigious an address that
roads bearing its name began popping up all over town:
Peachtree Street, West Peachtree Street, Peachtree Place, Peachtree
Road and Peachtree Center Avenue, just to name a few. The main
Peachtree Street runs from Little Five Points in downtown Atlanta
into Buckhead, where the name changes to Peachtree Road and
then to Peachtree Industrial Boulevard.

Willkommen

When white settlers replaced the Cherokee Natives who had
originally occupied Helen, a small town in the Blue Ridge
Mountains, the area lagged for a time. A strong and vibrant log-
ging industry took root in the early 1900s, which cleared much
of the virgin timber and then abandoned the area. This left
remaining residents scratching their heads over what to do to
prevent their community from becoming a ghost town. In 1968,
an artist presented a group of business people with the idea of
transforming Helen into an alpine haven, modeled after the
Bavarian villages he'd seen when he was stationed in Germany
during World War II. The idea was met with much enthusiasm,
and today, visiting Helen is like stepping into the Bavarian Alps.

Every year during Oktoberfest the area becomes packed with visitors who travel to the region to dine on authentic Bavarian food, drink beer and listen as the lederhosen-clad oompah bands play.

Montezuma's Revenge

Montezuma might seem a strange name for a town in Georgia, but it's not so surprising considering that the Native peoples who first settled there were said to be direct descendants of the Aztecs. When the city was incorporated in 1854, the Georgia legislature kept the name Montezuma, which had been given by the Natives in honor of the Mexican emperor. Incidentally, Montezuma has also been home to a thriving Mennonite community since several Mennonite families moved to the town from Virginia in the 1950s.

Stories Behind Other Place Names

☞ Americus—This town name was literally drawn from a hat. When the town was incorporated in 1932, commissioners wrote a bunch of names on slips of paper and put them into a hat. The name Americus—the masculine version of America—was picked.

☞ Beaver—Several small bodies of water in Georgia are named "beaver" (Beaver Creek, Beaver Ruin Creek, Beaver Pond), supposedly because of the large numbers of toothy rodents in those areas.

☞ Between—This town in Walton County was so named simply because it is quite literally in between Monroe and Loganville.

☞ Buckhead—Atlanta's ritziest neighborhood had very humble beginnings. In 1837, Henry Irby opened a general store and tavern at what is now the intersection of West Paces

Ferry Road and Roswell Road. As the story goes, Irby killed a large buck deer and placed its head in a prominent location, hence the name "buck head."

☛ Chamblee—The name of this town reportedly came from a petition sent to the U.S. Postal Service to establish a post office in a town called Roswell Junction. Because there already was a town with the name Roswell nearby, someone at the Postal Service arbitrarily chose the name Chamblee from the list of petitioners for the post office name.

☛ Chattahoochee River—The name "Chattahoochee" comes from the Creek words for "painted rock."

☛ Commerce—It used to be called Harmony Grove, but when the cotton industry took off, the name was changed in 1904 to reflect the town's growing prosperity.

☛ Hard Labor Creek—This stream in Morgan County gets its name either from the slaves who struggled to till the fields or the Native Americans who found the waters difficult to cross.

☛ Hooker—Get your mind out of the gutter! This town was actually named for Union general Joseph Hooker, who passed through during the Civil War.

☛ Ideal—It was named Joetown, until two railroad executives stopped there and one proclaimed the town an "ideal" place for a train stop. The other man was said to have exclaimed, "And you have just named it!"

☛ Lake Lanier—One of Georgia's favorite summer recreation spots, Lake Lanier was named after the 19th-century poet, Sidney Lanier, who wrote the famous poem, "Song of the Chattahoochee."

☛ Little Five Points—This artsy Atlanta neighborhood is in the center of the downtown hub, from which main roads branch out in all directions.

☛ Lookout Mountain—Although some say the name of this mountain, which extends into Tennessee and Alabama, originated with General Andrew Jackson's forces, it more likely comes from the Cherokee term for "two mountains looking at each other."

☛ Okefenokee Swamp—"Okefenokee" comes from the Seminole Native word for "land of trembling earth," likely because the floating islands deceivingly appear to be solid land. Over the years, "Okefenokee" has been spelled more than 70 different ways, including "Ekanifinaka," "Akenfonoga" and "Eckenfinooka."

☛ Piedmont—The name that comes from the French word for "foot of the mountain" graces an avenue, college, wildlife refuge, hospital and park, among other places, most of which are nowhere near a mountain.

☛ Santa Claus—Farmer Green came up with this name to attract tourists to his pecan orchard and motel. In keeping with the Christmas theme, the town has a Candy Cane Road, Rudolph Way and Sleigh Street.

DID YOU KNOW?

Locals in the Atlanta area are always asked whether they live "inside" or "outside" the Perimeter. They're referring to the ring formed by highway I-285 around metropolitan Atlanta (those in the know call it by its acronyms, "ITP" or "OTP"). And when they say "Spaghetti Junction," they mean the twirling tangle of overpasses where I-85 and I-285 meet.

Georgia Cities that Share their Names

Athens	Delhi	Macedonia
Berlin	Denmark	Mexico
Brooklyn	Dublin	Milan
Budapest	Egypt	Montreal
Cairo	Geneva	Paris
Cleveland	Glasgow	Quebec
Columbus	Harlem	Rome
Cuba	Kansas	Vienna
Damascus	Long Island	Warsaw

MEMORABLE MOMENTS

Shiver Me Timbers!

The Pirates House restaurant in Savannah was once a regular stop for sailors and pirates, who would drink their grog and recount their exploits on the high seas. The place was supposedly featured in Robert Louis Stevenson's novel *Treasure Island*, and Captain Flint was said to have died in one of its upstairs rooms. Some say that his ghost still haunts the halls on moonless nights.

Secret Meetings

Jekyll Island, the smallest of Georgia's barrier islands, played host to some pretty important gatherings in the late 1800s and early 1900s. It was the ultra-exclusive winter retreat of 53 prominent business leaders, including John D. Rockefeller, J.P. Morgan and William Vanderbilt. In November 1910, it was the site of meetings so secretive that the participants went only by their first names (they were termed the "First Name Club"). Among the six financial leaders who attended were Senator Nelson Aldrich, A. Piatt Andrew (assistant secretary of the treasury) and Henry P. Davison (partner in the firm of J.P. Morgan). Although the "first namers" claimed they were there on a duck-hunting excursion, they were actually developing a plan that ultimately formed the basis of the country's Federal Reserve System.

Stop in at the Whistle Stop

Juliette is home to the Whistle Stop Cafe, probably best known as the set of the 1991 film *Fried Green Tomatoes,* starring Jessica Tandy, Mary Stuart Masterson and Mary-Louise Parker. Edward L. Williams Sr. built the place in 1927 as a general merchandise store that sold everything from groceries to cattle feed. In 1972, Williams finally closed his doors, saying, "I have had enough." But since the movie brought so much attention to the site, the Whistle Stop has been reopened as a café, and of course, fried green tomatoes are the specialty of the house.

Georgia Gold

Two decades before thousands of people rushed out west to stake their claim in the California Gold Rush, Georgians were enjoying their own windfall. In 1828, Benjamin Parks discovered gold in Habersham County (the real credit for the first discovery is said to belong to Frank Logan in White County) and a year later, mining began there. The discovery sent thousands

of people scrambling into them thar north Georgia hills for a piece of the riches. Dahlonega was the center of gold production during the Georgia Gold Rush, and although the mines have long since ceased operation, visitors to the site can still pan for gold.

The top of the Georgia state capitol building in Atlanta owes its shine to the Georgia Gold Rush. In 1958, Dahlonega residents donated 43 ounces of gold, which were carried by mule-driven wagon to Atlanta and presented to then Governor Marvin Griffin. The gold was pounded to 1/5000 of an inch thick and installed on top of the capitol building.

For Sale: One Slightly Used Town

When actress and Georgia native Kim Basinger bought the town of Braselton for $20 million in 1989, some people scratched their heads in wonder, but the town's 500 residents were thrilled that she was putting their tiny city on the map. They were especially pleased when she announced plans to restore the downtown area and turn Braselton into a tourist attraction. But in 1993, after a contract dispute over the movie *Boxing Helena* forced her to fork over $8 million, Basinger declared bankruptcy and gave up her personal interest in Braselton.

A Cursed Town?

Was the town of Jacksonboro really cursed? Many Georgians believe it was. It all started when a traveling preacher named Lorenzo Dow passed through the town in around 1820. He had earned the name "Crazy Dow" for his fire-and-brimstone sermons. While delivering one of those sermons, Dow was harassed by a group of rowdies, who later began beating him. If it weren't for a man named Seaborn Goodall, Dow might have been killed. As he left town via a bridge over Beaver Dam Creek, Dow reportedly put a curse on the town. Eventually every structure in Jacksonboro either burned or was destroyed— except for Seaborn Goodall's house. Truth or fiction? You decide.

SHOW ME THE MONEY!

What You Get for the Price

The Atlanta metro area enjoys a slightly lower overall cost of living than the rest of the nation. Housing, utilities and grocery prices are all lower than the national average. Here are the prices you'd expect to pay in Georgia for these products and services:

Product/Service	Georgia	National Average
A new home	$170,000 (Atlanta area)	$212,300
Property taxes (per year)	$1050	$1632
Healthcare (per year)	$4891	$5247
Hospital stay (per day)	$1202	$1522
Gasoline	$2.70 per gallon	$2.80 per gallon
Electricity	7.79 cents per kilowatt hour	8.85 cents per kilowatt hour

Earnings Extremes

Georgia pays one of the lowest minimum wages in the country—a meager $5.15 an hour as of summer 2007. Yet the state is also home to the highest-earning county in the nation. Forsyth County is ranked number one in household income, with the average family bringing in $83,000 annually. Overall, Georgia households earn an average of $46,832 a year, slightly below the $48,451 national average.

Georgia Economy at a Glance

Here are some important facts and figures about living and working in Georgia:

☛ Georgia has a gross state product of $10 billion, making it the 10th biggest moneymaking state in the nation.

☛ Seventeen Fortune 500 companies have set up their corporate headquarters in Georgia, including the Home Depot, UPS, Coca-Cola and Delta Airlines.

☛ An estimated 4.8 million people work in the state.

☛ Most people are employed in business services, which make up 23 percent of Georgia jobs. Other big hiring sectors are trade, transportation and utilities (21 percent); manufacturing (11 percent); education and health (11 percent); and hospitality (9 percent).

☛ Georgia has a 4.6 percent unemployment rate, just slightly lower than the national average.

☛ Workers in the manufacturing industry bring home an average weekly salary of $567.84, among the lowest wages in the country.

☛ Georgia is a Right-to-Work state, which means that employees don't have to join a union, no matter where they work.

GETTIN' AROUND

By Air

No matter where in the world you have flown, there's a good chance you've stopped off in Atlanta on the way. The Hartsfield-Jackson Atlanta International Airport is the busiest in the nation, with about 85 million passengers moving through it in 2006. Thirty-two airlines operate more than 2600 flights per day, to 169 U.S. cities and 85 international cities. To accommodate the traffic, Hartsfield is undergoing a $5.4 billion makeover, adding a new rental car complex and international terminal and sprucing up its existing terminals.

Quick facts about Hartsfield:

☛ The terminal area measures 5.8 million square feet.

☛ The airport has an underground train system that runs on a 3.5-mile track. Trains arrive at the terminal stations once every two minutes.

☛ The airport has five runways. Three runways measure 9000 feet, one measures 10,000 feet, and one measures 11,889 feet.

☛ The airport has enough parking spaces to fit 29,334 cars.

☛ Hartsfield is the largest employment center in the state, with 56,000 employees earning $2.4 billion collectively each year.

Hartsfield is by far the biggest, but it isn't the only airport in Georgia. Albany, Athens, Columbus, Macon, Savannah and several other cities also have their own regional airports. In fact, the state has 103 public-use airports in all, as well as 245 private airports, 118 heliports and six military airports.

By Road

Georgia has about 114,000 miles of public roads and 15 interstates, which include the major routes I-20, I-75, I-85, I-95, I-575 and I-675.

Quick facts about Georgia's roads:

☛ I-95 runs along the East Coast, stretching nearly 2000 miles from Maine to Florida.

☛ I-75 bisects the state from north to south, from the Tennessee border to the Florida border.

☛ I-85 runs from the northeast corner of the state south to the Alabama border.

☛ I-20 runs across the state, from Alabama on the west to South Carolina on the east.

☛ If you're in a rush, bring a friend along. The Atlanta metro area has 18 miles of HOV (high occupancy vehicle) lanes along I-20, and 60 miles on·I-75/85. To ride in these lanes, you need to have at least two people in your car, an alternative fuel vehicle or a motorcycle. Don't try to sneak into an

HOV lane without a passenger, or you could be hit with a $75 fine.

☞ It's smooth driving along Georgia's roads—one study ranked the state as having the best pavement conditions in the country.

☞ Georgia had 6.9 million licensed drivers as of 2003.

☞ More than 331,000 motor vehicle crashes were recorded in 2003, resulting in over 1600 fatalities.

☞ For those who want to get in a bit of exercise and save on gas costs, the state has 14 official bicycle routes.

If you don't have a car, never fear—there are other options for getting around. The Metropolitan Atlanta Rapid Transit Authority (MARTA) offers train and bus service for Fulton and DeKalb Counties, as well as for the city of Atlanta. Cobb County Transit (CCT), Gwinnett Transit and Clayton County Transit (C-Tran) cover bus services in their respective areas.

DID YOU KNOW?

In March 2000, MARTA gave a ride to its 3.5 *billionth* passenger.

By Rail

Georgia has the vastest train system in the Southeast, with 4700 miles of railroads offering services to 500 cities and towns. MARTA and Amtrak trains carry passengers, whereas CSX and Norfolk-Southern handle most of the freight service.

Considering how quickly the state is growing, Georgia needs to increase its passenger train service. The Georgia Department of Transportation has undertaken a major effort to add seven commuter rail lines with 45 stations, as well as seven intercity rail lines. By the year 2030, an estimated 10.7 million commuters and 2.1 million intercity travelers will use these services.

By Sea

It's hard to imagine getting on a boat in this mostly landlocked state, but Georgia does have its ports. The Port of Savannah on the Savannah River is the second-largest container port on the East Coast, even though it is 21 miles inland from the Atlantic Ocean. The Port of Brunswick is the fourth-largest auto port in the country. It's about 12 miles from the ocean.

 The Central of Georgia railroad has been honored by several distinctions. It was the state's first railroad, established in 1833 by a group of businessmen known as the Central Railroad and Canal Company. At the time it was also the longest railroad in the world owned by one company (it ran 190 miles from Savannah to Macon). Finally, it was the longest running railroad in Georgia, although by the 1980s, it had been absorbed by the Norfolk Southern Company.

BUSINESS LEADERS

The Man Behind Coca-Cola

In 1923, 33-year-old Robert Woodruff was a successful vice president of the White Motor Company when he was offered a job at a struggling soft drink company in Atlanta called Coca-Cola. Woodruff's father, businessman W.C. Bradley, had purchased the company for $25 million in 1919, but it was floundering. Woodruff accepted the job, taking a $50,000 pay cut from his previous position. During his time there, he increased the company's bottling operations, introduced the six-bottle carton and turned Coca-Cola into one of the best known brands in the world.

When he turned 65 in 1955, Woodruff had to retire—that was the rule at Coca-Cola. But he stayed on as the company's leader, at least in spirit, until his death in 1985. After retiring, Woodruff focused on philanthropy, donating an unprecedented $105 million to Emory University in 1979 and helping to create the Robert W. Woodruff Arts Center in Atlanta.

Forward Atlanta

If it hadn't been for two men named Ivan Allen, Atlanta might not be the thriving city it is today. Ivan Allen Sr. was a prominent businessman who served as president of the Atlanta Chamber of Commerce and launched a campaign called "Forward Atlanta" to promote the city. His son was a two-term mayor who was instrumental in bringing the Braves, Hawks and Falcons to the city. Ivan Allen Jr. continued his father's "Forward Atlanta" campaign by promoting a building boom in which more than 50 new buildings went up, including the Memorial Arts Center and the Atlanta Civic Center. By the 1960s, 440 of *Fortune* magazine's top 500 companies had set up office in Atlanta.

Media Mogul

Although some take issue with his brash business style (he's been called "Mouth from the South"), Ted Turner changed the way the world watches television. In 1970, the young entrepreneur bought a small UHF television station in Atlanta. By the end of the decade he had turned it into the country's first "superstation"—Turner Broadcasting System (TBS)—beaming sports, sitcom reruns and movies into homes around the country. He followed it up with the 24-hour Cable News Network (CNN) in 1980. Although some wondered why anyone would want to watch the news at 3 AM, CNN's breaking coverage of the Gulf War and other major world events established it as one of the preeminent news organizations in the world. By 1995, CNN reached 156 million people in 140 countries. Turner's family of networks expanded to include Turner Network Television (TNT), Turner Classic Movies (TCM), SportSouth, and The Cartoon Network. Turner also made significant contributions to sports. He's owned both the Atlanta Braves and the Hawks, and he launched the Goodwill Games.

Over the years, Turner has been more than a media mogul—he's become a world-renowned humanitarian. In 1996, he sold his empire to Time Warner, and four years later he left its board to devote himself to other projects. In 1997, he pledged $1 billion to the United Nations. He has also launched the eco-friendly burger chain, Ted's Montana Grill, and has set up several foundations to carry out his many philanthropic endeavors.

Building an Empire

Getting fired from the Handy Dan discount drugstore chain in 1978 turned out to be the best thing that ever happened to Arthur Blank and Bernie Marcus. The two businessmen combined their talents and opened the Home Depot chain of home-improvement warehouses on June 22, 1979, making Atlanta the company's official headquarters. By 2005, Home Depot was the nation's second-biggest retailer (just behind Wal-Mart), and today it has more than 2100 stores throughout the U.S., Canada and Mexico.

Blank retired as co-chairman of Home Depot in 2001 and bought the Atlanta Falcons football team the following year for $545 million. Marcus retired in 2002 and donated $200 million to build the Georgia Aquarium.

GEORGIA GEMS   In 1946, Atlanta native Truett Cathy owned a restaurant so modest that it was called the Dwarf Grill (it had only four tables). In 1961, Cathy came up with a recipe that was as simple as it was genius—the pressure-cooked chicken breast sandwich. Six years later he opened the first Chick-fil-A restaurant in Atlanta's

Greenbriar Mall. The chain's "Eat More Chikin" cows have now mooed their way into more than 1200 restaurants in 38 states.

Cathy has given back to the community that helped make him such a success. He and his wife Jeannette have taken in more than 150 foster children. In 1984, he established a foundation that has created foster homes in Georgia, Tennessee, Alabama and Brazil, and provides scholarships to dozens of students each year.

AFLAC!

Just about everyone has heard of the talking duck who reminds consumers where to buy their supplemental insurance (AFLAC!), but they might not be as familiar with the company's founder. John Amos was born in Enterprise, Alabama, in 1924, and worked as a partner at Prudential Insurance Company before deciding to move to Columbus, Georgia, to start his own company. His American Family Life Insurance Company (better known as AFLAC) differentiated itself by offering specialty health insurance. When Amos died of lung cancer in 1990, he was worth an estimated $8 billion.

A Real Leader

He played an integral role in the civil rights movement, led a major corporation and was instrumental in bringing the Olympics to Atlanta. Jesse Hill was born in St. Louis, Missouri, and moved to Atlanta in 1949 to take a position with the Atlanta Life Insurance Company. During the '50s and '60s, he pushed for desegregation at Georgia's colleges and contributed significantly to Martin Luther King's civil rights efforts. In 1973, he became president and CEO of Atlanta Life Insurance, presiding over one of the most fertile periods in the company's history. In 1977, Hill became the first African American to serve as president of the Atlanta Chamber of Commerce.

STATE OF GEORGIA'S INDUSTRY

Wait One Cotton Pickin' Minute!

In the 1700s and 1800s, cotton was the staple crop in Georgia. But one tiny insect nearly wiped out the state's entire cotton industry. Boll weevils crawled their way out of Mexico and into the South in the first few years of the 20th century, and though they measured just a few millimeters across, they devastated some three million acres of Georgia's cotton crops within a few years. Boll weevils continued to torment cotton farmers until the late 1980s, when programs to combat the little critter finally worked.

DID YOU KNOW?

About 11 million acres of Georgia land is devoted to farming. The state is the number one producer of poultry, peanuts, pecans, eggs and rye, and the second-biggest producer of cotton in the nation.

Pulp Reality

The pulp and paper business in Georgia is nothing to sneeze at. Since 1927, the state has been home to the Georgia-Pacific Company, one of the world's largest manufacturers of tissues, paper, pulp and building products. Chances are you've wiped some part of your body with one of their products, which include Quilted Northern and Angel Soft toilet paper, Brawny and Sparkle paper towels and Vanity Fair napkins.

Cutting a Rug

Located just about an hour north of Atlanta, Dalton is such a prolific rug producer that it's the self-proclaimed "carpet capital of the world"—and with good reason. About 90 percent of the world's carpets are made within a 65-mile radius of the city. A century ago, the area had another name—"Bedspread Alley." That's because women in the area sold bedspreads to earn extra money. They hung the bedspreads in front of their homes to attract the travelers driving through the town from Atlanta to Chattanooga and back. But in the 1950s, the bedspread business started to go under. Not wanting to waste expensive machinery, companies converted the equipment used to make the bedspreads to produce carpets instead. With the rise in wall-to-wall carpeting in the '50s, the rug industry took off in Dalton, and it's been booming ever since.

WHO'S IN CHARGE?

Struggle for Political Control

In the early 1800s, two men—John Clark and George M. Troup—were locked in a bitter struggle for control of the Georgia political system. Clark was a former major general in the Georgia Militia and a member of the state's General Assembly. Troup was a former U.S. congressman and senator. The men first vied for governor in 1819. Troup's supporters in the contest were called Troupites, while Clark's were called Clarkites. Clark won the election, as well as elections in 1823 and 1825 (the state's first popular election). By the mid-1800s, Troupites went on to form the Georgia Whig Party; former backers of John Clark formed the Union Party.

We're Outta Here!

In the 1840s and '50s, political parties were deeply divided over the issue of slavery—even among themselves. Whereas northern Democrats wanted the states to make their own decisions about whether to allow slavery, the southern Democrats wanted the government to support slavery in the territories. Meanwhile, the Republican Party opposed the expansion of slavery in the new territories. When Republican Abraham Lincoln was elected to the presidency in 1860, the turmoil erupted and the southern states began to secede. Although the state was deeply divided on the issue, Georgians ultimately decided to secede on January 19, 1861, fifth in line behind South Carolina, Alabama, Mississippi and Florida.

DID YOU KNOW?

In 1868, a few short years after slavery was abolished, 32 African Americans were elected to the Georgia House and Senate.

Unfair!

In 1917, the Georgia legislature came up with a new method for counting votes in the state's elections. The county-unit system classified each of the state's 159 counties by population into one of three categories: urban, town or rural. Here's how the votes stacked up:

☞ The eight urban counties had six unit votes each.

☞ The 30 town counties had four unit votes each.

☞ The 121 rural counties had two unit votes each.

Basically, this system allowed the smallest counties in Georgia to rack up 242 votes, while the eight biggest counties combined had only 48. That meant a small county with only a few hundred people had the same voting power as a major city with thousands of residents. In 1963, a challenge to the system went all the way to the Supreme Court, at which time the county-unit system met its demise.

Challenging Democratic Rule

For much of its history, Georgia has solidly been under Democratic control; in fact, so much so, that many gubernatorial elections in the 19th and early 20th century were non-events. That changed in 1966 when the Republicans made a serious run for the governor's office, leading to one of the most bizarre gubernatorial elections in the state's history. Running on the Democratic ticket were Ellis Arnall, the progressive former Democratic governor (1943–47); Lester Maddox, a known segregationist and fierce opponent of the civil rights movement; and liberal Senator Jimmy Carter. Their Republican opponent was Howard Hollis "Bo" Callaway, who was looking to become the first Republican governor of Georgia since 1872.

In the Democratic primary, Arnall received only 29 percent of the votes and was forced into a runoff with Maddox, which

Maddox won. Upset at the thought of having to choose between two conservative candidates, Georgia voters organized a write-in campaign to get Arnall's name on the final ballot. Although Callaway ended up with the most popular votes, no single candidate ended up with the majority vote, so by Georgia law, the Georgia General Assembly got to choose the governor. The Democratic-controlled legislature chose the conservative Maddox by a vote of 182 to 66.

The State of Georgia Politics

Here are a few important facts about Georgia's government:

☛ To be elected governor in Georgia, a person must be at least 30 years old and must have been a U.S. citizen for 15 years and a Georgia resident for six years. Governors serve a four-year term and can't stay in office for more than two terms.

☛ In addition to the governor, there are seven other elected executive officers: lieutenant governor, secretary of state, attorney general, commissioner of agriculture, commissioner of labor, commissioner of insurance, and superintendent of schools.

☞ The Georgia General Assembly has been the legislative branch of Georgia government since 1777 (it's older than the U.S. Congress). It's composed of a Senate, which has 56 members, and a House of Representatives, which has 180 members.

☞ The state's judicial system is made up of two main appellate courts: the Supreme Court and the Court of Appeals. They don't try cases, but they do hear appeals from lower courts. Trial courts are divided into 48 circuits, which are overseen by one or more judges.

☞ The local government consists of counties, cities and special districts. Counties handle elections, roads, health and auto-mobile licenses. Cities are run by a mayor and city council. Special districts operate specific services, such as public schools, airports and public transit.

DID YOU KNOW?

As the suffrage movement gained momentum, Georgia was left in the dust when it rejected the constitutional amendment allowing women to vote. Fortunately, the state had no choice but to follow along when the Amendment was ratified on August 18, 1920. Women began voting in Georgia during the 1920 election.

NOTABLE POLITICIANS

Thomas E. Watson

One of the most controversial figures in Georgia politics, this congressman and senator led Georgia's Populist movement in the late 1800s. Although early in his career he championed programs such as free rural mail delivery and public education, and he condemned lynching, he became increasingly racist in his later years. In 1908, he ran for president as a white supremacist. An equal opportunity offender, Watson also took potshots at the Catholic Church.

One-Eyed Plowboy

Georgia governor Allen D. Candler, sometimes called the "one-eyed plowboy of Pigeon Roost," lost his left eye in the Civil War battle at Jonesboro. But that didn't stop him from having a successful political career. He served as mayor of Gainesville, senator and secretary of state, before being elected governor in 1898. When he retired, Candler turned record-keeper, compiling many volumes of the state's Colonial, Revolutionary War and Confederate records. Candler County was named in his honor.

DID YOU  KNOW?

Rebecca Latimer Felton holds the records for the first woman to serve in the U.S. Senate, the oldest senator (she was 87) and the shortest senate term in history. She started her senate term on November 21, 1922, to replace the recently deceased Senator Tom Watson. Her term ended just 24 hours later, when Senator-Elect Walter F. George stepped in to fill the seat. Fortunately, Felton was famous for other things—particularly as a champion of women's rights.

Under His Wing, Georgia Takes Flight

The busiest airport in the world bears his name, thanks to William B. Hartsfield's invaluable contributions to the airline industry. Hartsfield served for six terms as Atlanta's mayor, longer than any other mayor in the city's history. In 1922, while still a city councilman, and just as the airline business was taking off, Hartsfield had the foresight to set aside 287 acres south of Atlanta for Candler Field, a landing strip that eventually grew into the city's international airport. When Hartsfield died in 1971, the Atlanta City Council honored the man who became known as Atlanta's "Father of Aviation," by renaming the airport the William B. Hartsfield Atlanta International Airport. Today it's known as Hartsfield-Jackson Atlanta International Airport, to also honor former mayor Maynard Jackson.

And Speaking of Jackson...
He was the first African American mayor to be elected in a major southern city, and at just 35, Maynard Jackson was the youngest mayor in the city's history. During his three terms in office, he built the enormous terminal at Hartsfield Atlanta Airport, helped minority businesses move forward and was instrumental in bringing the Olympics to Atlanta in 1996. When Jackson died in 2003, his name was added to Atlanta's airport. At the funeral, former President Bill Clinton noted that Jackson had a "voice that could melt the meanness out of the hardest heart" and a "gift of gab that could talk an owl out of a tree."

The Wild Man
Eugene Talmadge was one of the most controversial figures in Georgia politics. A vehement opponent of both Roosevelt's New Deal and civil rights, and so radically right wing that he earned the nickname "The Wild Man from Sugar Creek," Talmadge was nevertheless able to get elected to the governor's office not once but four times (in 1932, 1934, 1940 and 1946)—although he only served three of his terms. Just before his inauguration, on December 21, 1946, Talmadge died.

Will the Real Governor Step Forward

Talmadge's death led to one of the strangest moments in Georgia politics, which came to be known as "The Three Governors Controversy." His supporters convinced the Georgia legislature to put Talmadge's son, Herman, into the governor's seat. The only problem was that the sitting governor, Ellis Arnall, refused to leave office. So Talmadge grabbed a .38 caliber Smith and Wesson, seized control of the office and changed the locks on the door. Not dismissed so easily, Arnall set up his office in an information booth in the capitol. Meanwhile, the 1946 election had added the new position of lieutenant governor, which was filled by Melvin Thompson, who said *he* held the rightful claim to the governor's office. Finally, in March 1947, the Georgia Supreme Court ruled in favor of Thompson, and only one governor was left standing. Thompson's rule didn't last long, though. Herman Talmadge challenged him in a 1948 special election and won. Talmadge served as governor from 1948 to 1955.

Peanut Farmer for President

Who'd have thought that a peanut farmer from Plains, Georgia, would go on to become the nation's 39th president? Jimmy Carter served two terms in the state legislature (1963–67) and one term as governor (1971–75) before running for president in 1975. The "peanut farmer from Georgia" beat the odds in 1976 and defeated Republican incumbent Gerald R. Ford to become the first-ever U.S. president from the state of Georgia. During his presidency, Carter led the historic Camp David agreement in 1978, which helped bring peace between Israel and Egypt. Ultimately, though, the Iranian Hostage Crisis cost him a second term in the 1980 election. Carter went on to become one of the most successful ex-presidents in history, working tirelessly to promote human rights around the world. He was awarded the Nobel Peace Prize in 2002 for his efforts.

Courting Controversy

She has smacked an officer and insinuated that President Bush knew about the terrorist attacks of September 11 beforehand and did nothing to stop them. Cynthia McKinney has become known as much, if not more, for her explosive statements as for her political leadership. During a 1996 Congressional campaign, for example, she called her political opponents' supporters "a ragtag group of neo-Confederates."

In 2001, New York mayor Rudy Giuliani refused a Saudi prince's $10 million donation for victims of the September 11 attack. Because the prince had suggested the U.S.'s Middle East policy had something to do with the terrorist acts, Giuliani sent back the check, but McKinney was quick to jump on it. She wrote the prince a three-page letter, asking for a share of the dough to help African Americans in need. Then in 2006, McKinney whacked a Capitol police officer when he tried to stop her from entering the building without proper ID. Voters spoke back in 2006, and McKinney was sent out of office.

Switching Sides

And speaking of controversy, former governor Zell Miller sparked one of his own when he addressed the Republican National Convention in 2004. The lifelong Democrat railed against his party, denouncing their "warped way of thinking" and "manic obsession to bring down our commander in chief." Although many Republicans praised the switcheroo, Democrats were not so pleased.

CRIME AND PUNISHMENT

Crime Stats

Do you need to hold your pocketbook more tightly when you're walking Georgia's streets? Overall, the state ranks 20th in crime, putting it just above average on the list of the nation's most dangerous states. Here are the real numbers on Georgia's crime rates in 2006:

- ☞ Murders: 601
- ☞ Rapes: 1992
- ☞ Robberies: 14,753
- ☞ Aggravated Assaults: 23,841
- ☞ Auto thefts: 40,817
- ☞ Burglaries: 78,578

Strange Laws

Georgia has its share of bizarre legislation. These are just a few of the laws and ordinances on the books that make you wonder, "What were they thinking?":

- ☞ In Kennesaw, every household must own at least one gun and the proper ammunition. The law has been on the books since 1982, and it has reportedly led to a drop in crime.

- ☞ It's a massager, officer, honest! Any type of sex toy that stimulates one's "naughty parts" is strictly off-limits in the state.

- Speaking of sex, it's also technically illegal to do the deed if you're not married.

- Even if the deceased owed you money, hold your tongue at his funeral. By law, you can't curse in front of a dead body.

- The chicken better not cross the road in Quitman—it's against the law. Actually, the ordinance was created to prevent farmers from letting their chickens, ducks and geese run wild.

- No matter how excited you are, don't get caught saying "Oh boy!" in Jonesboro, or you could be in big trouble.

- If you're ever in Conyers and have a hankering for "two fried eggs and a fritter for a quarter," don't say it. This phrase has been banned in the city since about the early 1900s. It started when Emory University students used to ride the special train through town on their way to and from school. When the train stopped at Conyers, food vendors got on, including an African American woman who sold food using this trademark phrase. The students mimicked her, shouting, "Two fried eggs and a fritter for a quarter!" until the residents of Conyers got fed up. One day in May 1902, when the students yelled out the phrase, they got just what they asked for—they were hit with a shower of eggs. To put an end to the fighting, the Conyers City Council made it illegal both to say "two fried eggs and a fritter for a quarter" and to throw eggs at anyone.

☛ You can't keep any native Georgian species of lizard or snake as a pet, but you can keep a poisonous snake.

☛ If you're in need of a haircut, you'll have to wait to ask the price until you get in the chair, because barbers in the state are forbidden from advertising their prices.

☛ Slap someone on the back—or front—in Georgia and you could be in big trouble with the law.

DID YOU KNOW?

It's illegal to eat chicken with a fork in Gainesville.

GEORGIA'S MOST WANTED

The Leo Frank Case

On April 27, 1913, the beaten and strangled body of 13-year-old Mary Phagan was found in the basement of the National Pencil Factory where she had worked. Several men were arrested for the crime, including Newt Lee, the night watchman who discovered Phagan's body; Jim Conley, a sweeper at the factory; and Leo Frank, the superintendent. Although the evidence was largely circumstantial, Frank was found guilty of the murder and sentenced to hang. Two days before Frank was to die, Governor John M. Slaton commuted the sentence to life in prison. By then the case had garnered so much attention that the public was convinced of Frank's guilt and outraged by the reduced sentenced. On August 16, 1915, an angry mob pulled Frank from his cell and lynched him from a Marietta tree.

Child Murders

It was one of the most grizzly crime sprees in Atlanta's history. Twenty-nine African American boys and young men disappeared or were found murdered from 1979 to 1981. In 1982, Wayne Williams was convicted of killing the last two men, Nathaniel Carter, 27, and Jimmy Ray Payne, 21, and was given two consecutive life sentences. Williams has never officially been tied to the other murders, however, and many people believe he was railroaded into a charge so the FBI could close the case. In 2005, DeKalb County Police Chief Louis Graham reopened four of the cases, saying that he believed in Williams' innocence.

Garden of Evil

Savannah is normally a tranquil city. But one night in May 1984, the calm was ripped by the sound of gunfire. In the famous Mercer House, antiques dealer Jim Williams shot and killed hustler Danny Hansford. Williams claimed he was acting in self-defense. He was tried four times over the course of eight years before finally being acquitted. Was it really murder, or self-defense as Williams claimed? The truth died with Williams in 1990. But some people believe he hasn't gone far. Lights have been seen on in his home when no one was there, and some people claim they witnessed Williams wandering in one of the homes he renovated. The famous murder was immortalized in the book and movie *Midnight in the Garden of Good and Evil*.

A Supernatural Crime

On October 24, 1994, Tina Resch was sentenced in a Carroll County courthouse for the murder of her three-year-old daughter, Amber. What made this crime so bizarre was the history of its perpetrator. When Tina was a teenager in 1984, strange things went on in her home. Radios and televisions turned on by themselves, lights switched on and off, bottles broke, kitchen chairs jumped around and pans flew through the air. When paranormal researchers came to investigate the disturbances, some thought Tina had real telekinetic powers, but others claimed she was just a disturbed young woman who was pulling a hoax. Although Resch proclaimed her innocence in the death of her child, she was sentenced to life in prison.

Cruel Crematorium

When the furnace at Tri-State Crematory in Noble broke in 1996, owner Ray Brent Marsh didn't shut down his business or get it fixed. Instead, he gave the grieving families urns of cement dust, took their money and piled their relatives' bodies into storage sheds, the woods and the lake behind his house. Investigators eventually found 334 bodies on his property,

many of which were so decomposed that they had turned into "biological soup," according to one forensic investigator. Marsh was eventually charged with 787 felony counts, including theft, abuse of a corpse and making false statements. He was sentenced in 2004 to 12 years in prison.

Murder on Steroids

He was a 2004 World Wrestling Entertainment heavyweight and Intercontinental wrestling champion, seemingly at the top of his game. But what pro wrestler Chris Benoit did one weekend in June 2007 was as baffling as it was horrifying. It is believed that at some point on Friday night, Benoit asphyxiated his wife, Nancy. Then on Saturday, he killed his seven-year-old son, Daniel, and then hanged himself from a weight machine in the basement of his Fayetteville home. What caused Benoit, who reportedly adored his wife and son, to snap that weekend? Some say it was "roid rage" caused by abuse of steroids, but others believe the frequent blows he suffered in the wrestling ring left him mentally impaired.

The Antifreeze Killer

Knives, guns, ropes...they've all been used as murder weapons...
but antifreeze? In 2007, Lynn Turner was convicted of murder-
ing her boyfriend, Forsyth County firefighter Randy Thompson,
with ethylene glycol, an ingredient in antifreeze. But wait,
there's more. At the time of her conviction, Turner was already
in jail for the 1995 murder of her husband, police officer Glen
Turner, by the same method. Turner has maintained her innocence in both cases, but the juries didn't buy it. She's serving
a life sentence without parole.

The Real Olympic Park Bomber

Atlanta worked hard to earn the right to host the Olympics, and
it was a proud moment when the events finally kicked off in the
summer of 1996. But the celebration came to a screeching halt
when a bomb ripped through Centennial Olympic Park in
downtown Atlanta, killing one person and injuring more than
100. Security guard Richard Jewell was quickly hailed as a hero
for moving crowds away from the suspicious package just
moments before it exploded, but soon the FBI's investigation
began to focus on him. It took months for the FBI to realize
Jewell wasn't the perpetrator, and nearly seven years for them to
track down the real bomber—Eric Robert Rudolph. Jewell eventually cleared his name and won hefty settlements against several news organizations for ruining his reputation. Finally
vindicated, Jewell died in August 2007 of health complications
caused by diabetes and kidney failure. As for the real Olympic
Park bomber, Rudolph is serving four consecutive life sentences
plus 120 years in prison.

The Runaway Bride

In the 1999 movie *Runaway Bride,* Julia Roberts played a
commitment-phobe with a tendency to lace up her running
shoes and take off just moments before reaching the altar. Six
years later, life imitated art when Atlanta bride-to-be Jennifer

Wilbanks dashed out on her betrothed just days before their wedding. The strange twist in the case was that Wilbanks disappeared while jogging near her home in Duluth and let her fiancée and family believe for several days that she had been kidnapped. It turned out that she had hopped a Greyhound bus across the country to Las Vegas and then Albuquerque, New Mexico, cutting her hair along the way so that she wouldn't be recognized. When police finally tracked Wilbanks down, she said that she had just "needed some time alone." Fiancée John Mason at first stuck by his runaway bride, but he finally called it quits about a year later. Ironically, Wilbanks sued her ex-fiancée in 2005, claiming that Mason owed her a share of the $500,000 he earned for selling their story.

On a Rampage

On a routine Friday morning in March 2005, Fulton County Superior Court Judge Rowland Barnes was hurrying a couple of attorneys along so he could finish up their case and move on. Suddenly there was a loud "bang!" and the judge slumped over, dead. His murderer was 33-year-old Brian Nichols, a defendant in a rape trial who had escaped by overpowering his female guard and stealing her weapon. Nichols then continued his shooting rampage, killing court reporter Julie Ann Brandau, Fulton County sheriff's deputy Hoyt Teasley, and federal agent David Wilhelm before disappearing into the city streets. Atlanta remained in virtual lockdown for more than a day as law enforcement agents conducted the biggest manhunt in Georgia's history. Nichols was finally captured in the apartment of a single mom named Ashley Smith, who was able to keep him calm by talking to him until police arrived.

Barbie Bandits

On a winter day in 2007, two bank robbers walked into a Bank of America in Acworth, handed over a note demanding cash and walked out with $11,000. What made this robbery so unusual was the grainy surveillance video of the crime. The two giggly blonde girls with designer sunglasses and tight jeans in the video looked more like Hollywood starlets than bank robbers, so much so that the media dubbed them the "Barbie Bandits." Although they made off with the cash, they were quickly nabbed after they went on a shopping spree at Gucci and had their hair done at an upscale salon. When the police picked them up, Ashley Nicole Miller and Heather Lyn Johnston, both 19, admitted to having committed the crime with the help of two male bank employees.

FORMAL LEARNING COMES TO GEORGIA

Baby Steps to Public Education

In 1821, the state legislature made the first steps toward a public education system. It authorized $750,000 to be spent on a "poor school fund" to provide schooling for the poorest residents. Still, this system wasn't widely accepted, and public education faltered. The public school system didn't officially launch in Georgia until October 1870.

Gustavus J. Orr

The man known as the "father" of public education in Georgia, Gustavus J. Orr, was elected as the state school commissioner in 1872. He pushed for school funding and urged the Georgia legislature to give the fledgling public school system a chance. The public schools flourished under his leadership, and he kept his position until his death in 1887.

DID YOU  KNOW?

In 1873, approximately 32,000 children attended Georgia's new public schools. The average school year was only 66 days, compared to about 180 days today.

Black and White

By the 1940s, Georgia was a segregated state. Black people were forced to sit in the back of buses, use separate bathrooms and even drink from different water fountains than white people. The same went for the state's schools. Even after the Supreme Court voted unanimously to end segregation in the nation's public schools in 1954, Georgia governor Marvin Griffin was insolent, declaring, "Come hell or high water, races will not be mixed in Georgia schools!" Eventually bigotry lost out, and in 1961, the first two black students were admitted to the University of Georgia. By the 1970s, nearly all of the public schools and colleges in Georgia had been integrated.

Dropping Out

Georgia students are tuning out and dropping out at some of the highest rates in the country. The state falls at the bottom of the list when it comes to high school graduation rates, with only about 61 percent making it through public high school.

But there is HOPE…

One program is giving Georgia's students plenty of "HOPE" for their future. Helping Outstanding Pupils Educationally (HOPE) was started in 1993, and since then, the scholarship program has doled out more than $3 billion in financial assistance to about 900,000 college students. The program pays full tuition at public colleges and universities and about $3000 per year for private schools. Every time people buy a Georgia lottery ticket, they're helping to fund this important program (and they might just get rich at the same time!).

GEORGIA PUBLIC SCHOOL SYSTEM AT A GLANCE

Fast Facts about Georgia's Schools

☛ Georgia has approximately 1.6 million students in about 2000 public schools, and they are educated by more than 97,000 teachers.

☛ The Georgia Department of Education oversees all public educational programs in the state.

☛ The Georgia Board of Education is run by a State School Superintendent.

☛ The average SAT score in the state in 2003–04 was 981, below the national average of 1017.

☛ When it comes to paying public school teachers, nationally, Georgia ranks 18th on the list, with teachers having an average salary of $46,526.

OFF TO COLLEGE

University of Georgia

When it was incorporated in 1785, the University of Georgia was the first state-supported university in the nation. John Milledge, a friend of Thomas Jefferson's and a future Georgia governor, purchased 633 acres from land speculator Daniel Easley for $4000 and gave it to the university trustees. Abraham Baldwin, one of the four Georgia men who signed the U.S. Constitution, was named as its president. Today, the University of Georgia has about 33,000 students.

Famous alumni: Governor Sonny Perdue, TV journalist Deborah Norville, Senators Saxby Chambliss and Johnny Isakson as well as A.D. "Pete" Correll (Georgia-Pacific Corporation Chairman of the Board).

Georgia Institute of Technology

Opened in 1888, "Georgia Tech" was, and still is, the school of choice for students pursuing degrees in science and engineering. Its 400-acre campus is home each year to about 16,000 students, and it consistently ranks among *U.S. News & World Report*'s top 10 public universities in the country. Georgia Tech is also known for its sports. Its Yellow Jackets have won four national college football titles and 15 conference crowns.

Famous alumni: President Jimmy Carter, Kary Mullis (Nobel Prize–winning scientist), Joe Rodgers Sr. (co-founder of The Waffle House restaurant chain), Ivan Allen Jr. (former Atlanta mayor), Michael Arad (architect of the World Trade Center Memorial in New York City) and Jeff Foxworthy (comedian).

Georgia State University

The second-largest school in the state, Georgia State University has a student population of 27,000 from around the nation and more than 145 different countries. It began in 1913 as an evening school to accommodate the educational needs of Atlanta's full-time employees but expanded in the late 1950s, and today offers more than 200 different majors.

Famous alumni: Paul Coverdell (former Georgia senator), James Copeland (former CEO of Deloitte Touche Tohmatsu), Julia Roberts (actress) and Jody Powell (former White House Press Secretary).

Emory University

In 1834, Georgia Methodists established a preparatory school on 400 acres of land in Newton County. Two years later, the Georgia legislature granted a charter to Emory College, which was named for Methodist bishop John Emory who had died in 1835 in a carriage accident. The college had strict rules. Students in the late 1800s were forbidden from "attending any ball, theatre, horse-race or cock-fight," "using intoxicating drinks," "playing cards" and "associating with persons of known bad character." In 1914, Coca-Cola Company founder Asa Candler offered the college $1 million and 72 acres of land to set up residence in Atlanta. The company again added to the school's coffer in 1979, when it gave $105 million in Coca-Cola stock, which was at the time the largest single gift to an American university. The financial contributions helped make Emory one of the most respected liberal arts colleges in the country, with nine schools and the state's largest healthcare system.

Famous alumni: David Brinkley (TV journalist), Max Cleland (former U.S. senator), Kenneth Cole (clothing designer) and Newt Gingrich (former United States Speaker of the House).

DID YOU KNOW?

During one week every spring on the Emory University campus, a strange skeletal figure dressed in black appears. Dooley, or the "spirit of Emory," makes a grand entrance every year—he has ridden in on a motorcycle, landed in a helicopter, and has even risen out of his own grave. Dooley is always accompanied by a group of student "bodyguards," armed with a water pistol and called by the first and middle initial of the current university president. The week culminates with Dooley's Ball, held in the center of campus.

Morehouse College

Georgia has a strong tradition of African American colleges and universities, including Spelman College and Clark Atlanta University. Morehouse College, a private liberal arts college for African American men, was founded in 1867 by Baptist minister, Reverend William Jefferson White, and former slave, Reverend Richard C. Coulter. At first, the school was named the Augusta Institute and was run out of church basements in Augusta and Atlanta. In 1885, it was moved to its current location three miles from downtown Atlanta, and in 1913 it was renamed Morehouse College in honor of Henry L. Morehouse, the corresponding secretary of the Northern Baptist Home Mission Society.

Famous alumni: Martin Luther King Jr., Edwin Moses (Olympic gold medal winner), Maynard Jackson (Atlanta mayor), Samuel L. Jackson (Academy Award–nominated actor) and Spike Lee (filmmaker).

Agnes Scott College

Ranked as one of the best colleges for women in the country, Agnes Scott actually started with a higher purpose. In 1889, Decatur Presbyterian Church Pastor Frank H. Gaines opened the Decatur Female Seminary with just 63 students. Church

member George Washington Scott donated $40,000 to the school, with the provision that it be named after his mother, Agnes. The Gothic and Victorian buildings are so stately that the college earned the distinction of being the fourth most beautiful college campus in the country on the 2007 Princeton Review Best 361 Colleges list.

Famous alumni: Jennifer Nettles (lead singer of the band Sugarland), Marsha Norman (Pulitzer Prize–winning playwright) and Katherine "Kay" Krill (CEO of Ann Taylor stores).

Spelman College

Morehouse's counterpart for women was also born in a church basement and founded by Baptists—Frank Quarles, pastor of Atlanta's Friendship Baptist Church, and missionaries Sophia B. Packard and Harriet E. Giles. The school was started in 1881 with just $100 in funding from the church and 11 students. Thanks to a generous donation from industrialist John D. Rockefeller, the school was moved two years later to its current location in Atlanta. The hit 1980s TV show *A Different World* was set at Hillman College, a school modeled after Spelman. Its creator, Bill Cosby, gave a generous $20 million donation to Spelman the following decade.

Famous alumni: Marian Wright Edelman (founder of the Children's Defense Fund), Alice Walker (Pulitzer Prize–winning novelist) and Keshia Knight Pulliam (actress on *The Cosby Show*).

Savannah College of Art and Design
The moss-draped squares of Savannah serve as the perfect backdrop for the nation's largest art and design school. Founded in 1978, Savannah College of Art and Design (or SCAD, as it's known) has been preparing students from around the globe for a career in the visual arts. The school hosts about 7000 students each year on its three campuses (Savannah, Atlanta and Lacoste, France).

Famous alumni: India Arie (Grammy award–winning R&B singer), Layne Brightwell (Hollywood costume designer), Mark Brooks (comic book artist) and Michael Scoggins (painter).

Wesleyan College
In the 1800s, educational opportunities for women were few and far between. In 1836, Wesleyan College in Macon became the first women's college in the world. It is also the birthplace of two sororities, the Adelphean Society in 1851 (now Alpha Delta Pi), and the Philomathean Society in 1852 (now Phi Mu). The school was way ahead of its time, schooling women in the sciences, as well as in history and languages.

Famous alumni: Neva Jane Langley Fickling (Miss America 1953), Sandra Deer (playwright) and Toni Jennings (the first female lieutenant governor of Florida).

Equal Education for All

By the 1960s, high school students in Georgia had many colleges from which to choose. But that wasn't the case for African American students. Colleges at the time were still segregated, until a man named Hamilton Holmes helped change that. Born in Atlanta in 1941, Holmes grew into an excellent student, graduating as valedictorian of his high school class. But when he and another student from his high school, Charlayne Hunter, applied to the University of Georgia in 1959, they were denied. Every quarter the two resubmitted their applications, only to be rejected again.

Finally, in 1961, a judge in Athens heard the case and decided that the only thing stopping the students from getting accepted was the color of their skin. The University of Georgia immediately accepted Holmes and Hunter, but the same could not be said for their fellow students. On their first day of class, the pair was taunted by students who shouted, "Two, four, six, eight. We don't want to integrate!" Holmes prevailed, though, graduating with honors in 1963. He went on to become the first African American student admitted to the Emory University School of Medicine.

VOILA! GREAT DISCOVERIES

Sweet Dreams

The drink that's been served to billions of people in nearly 200 countries would have been nothing but a fizzy dream if it hadn't been for a chemist from Knoxville, Georgia. In 1886, John Pemberton came up with a syrup made from the leaf of Peruvian coca and the cola nut. Pemberton's business partner, Frank Robinson, named the new drink "Coca-Cola." When Pemberton brought his syrup to Jacobs Pharmacy in Atlanta, they proclaimed it "excellent," added carbonated water to it and sold it as a fountain drink for five cents a glass. Pemberton began selling his syrup to pharmacies around the state. Alas, just as Coca-Cola was taking off, Pemberton died of stomach cancer on August 16, 1888.

Eli Whitney

Cotton was plentiful in antebellum Georgia. But what the state lacked was an efficient way to harvest the crop—until an inventor named Eli Whitney came along. While working as a private tutor on a Georgia plantation, Whitney learned that it took workers 10 hours to pull a single "point" of cotton lint from its surrounding seeds. Whitney came up with a machine called the "cotton gin" that, when cranked by hand, moved the cotton fiber through wire slots and separated out the seeds. He patented his invention in March 1794. The cotton gin expedited the cotton harvesting process and led to great prosperity for the state. However, because of constant legal battles, Whitney himself saw little profit from his invention and eventually left the South in disgust.

Dr. Charles H. Herty

Without the contributions of this Milledgeville-born chemist, you might not be reading this book. Herty pioneered a technology using the southern pine to make paper more cheaply than was being done in the 1800s, and he paved the way for Georgia's multi-million dollar paper industry.

Ongoing Research in Brief

Here are a few of the local research endeavors that might be tomorrow's big breakthroughs:

☛ Scientists at the University of Georgia have trained wasps that could serve as envoys in the war on terror by sniffing out explosives and poison at airports, border crossings and other high-security areas.

☛ They fly and crawl like bugs, but these creatures are completely mechanical. Robert Michelson and his team at the Georgia Institute of Technology Aerospace Laboratory are developing a tiny machine called an entomopter, which they hope to fly into places where humans can't go—Mars, for

example. The entomopter's wings beat with the help of a tiny chemical-generated "muscle."

☛ And speaking of flight, other researchers at Georgia Tech are working on a plane powered by a hydrogen fuel cell. The entire plane runs on less than 500 watts of energy—1/100th the power of the average hybrid car. Currently the plane is unmanned, but the researchers are hoping that their prototype will lead to bigger fuel-cell-powered aircraft.

If you're dreading bifocals, have hope: scientists at Georgia Tech have developed glasses that change focus like an auto-focus camera to adjust for differences in vision.

FAMOUS SCIENTISTS

Truly Stellar

After graduating from Georgia Tech with a degree in aeronautical engineering, Richard Truly went on to a stellar career. He became a NASA astronaut in 1969 and served as capsule communicator for all three manned Skylab missions and the Apollo-Soyuz mission in the 1970s. His first space mission was in November 1981, when Truly piloted the space shuttle *Columbia*. Later, he served as commander of the space shuttle *Challenger*. After the *Challenger* exploded while taking off in 1986, Truly took over as NASA administrator and helped rebuild the struggling space shuttle program.

Georgia's Nature Trail

Before America had even become an official nation, Philadelphia-born naturalist William Bartram helped map out its wildest stretches. From 1773 to 1776, he traveled through eight southern states, making notes in his journals all along the way. While in Georgia, Bartram discovered a new type of tree, which he named for his friend, Benjamin Franklin (Franklin tree or Franklinia alatamatha). Bartram's writings inspired authors Henry David Thoreau and William Wordsworth, and they endure as some of the finest natural accounts ever recorded. Today, visitors to North Georgia can retrace Bartram's footsteps by walking the 37-mile trail that stretches from the west fork of the Chattooga River over the summit of Rabin Bald to the North Carolina border.

Storm Warning

His was the quiet yet authoritative voice that for nearly 20 years warned Americans about impending hurricanes. John Hope joined the Atlanta-based *The Weather Channel* in 1982 as an on-camera meteorologist. He was such an expert in his specialty that other meteorologists called Hope "the man America watches" when hurricanes threatened. Sadly, in 2002 Hope died of heart problems at age 83.

HOW WELL ARE GEORGIA'S RESIDENTS?

Life Is Short

That's especially true if you live in Georgia. The state ranks way down at number 41 on the nation's life expectancy list, with the average resident surviving a mere 75.3 years.

Health Report Card

How does Georgia break down on health issues? Here's a look:

☞ Watch the fried chicken and barbecue ribs! Heart disease is the number-one killer in the state, responsible for 30 percent of all deaths in Georgia. That figure is 14 percent higher than the national average. All that good eating is also contributing to some serious weight gain. Almost half of all Georgia third graders are either overweight or obese, and the state ranks 14th overall in obesity.

☞ About 17 percent of residents don't have health insurance coverage.

☞ The good news is that Georgia's children are being protected against deadly diseases such as polio and measles. The state ranks third highest in the nation for childhood immunization coverage.

☞ You can breathe easier, because in 2005, Georgia banned smoking in restaurants, offices and other public places. The number of smokers in the state is well below the national average.

DID YOU KNOW?

About 12,000 babies are born in Georgia each year.

CONTROLLING DISEASE

The CDC

The nation's leading health research organization is headquartered in Atlanta. The Centers for Disease Control and Prevention, or CDC, has been around since 1946. Back then, it was called the Communicable Disease Center, and its primary goal was to destroy the pesky mosquitoes that cause malaria. Today, the CDC hunts down disease wherever it hides and helps protect Americans and people abroad. Some of the organization's greatest accomplishments:

☞ Helped wipe out smallpox

☞ Identified the Ebola virus

☞ Discovered how the hepatitis B virus was transmitted

☞ Identified toxic shock syndrome

The CDC has 12 different centers, including the National Center for Health Statistics, the National Center for Infectious Diseases and the National Center for Injury Prevention and Control. It operates under the umbrella of the Department of Health and Human Services and employs about 14,000 people in 10 U.S. states and in 46 countries around the world.

GREAT INVENTIONS

What a Gas!

Surgery in the old days was not a pleasant experience—patients were wide awake and could feel every excruciating incision. Then came Crawford Long, a country doctor from Danielsville. Long had seen traveling showmen make people giddy with "laughing gas," and he noticed that the people who'd taken this gas felt no pain. While in medical school, Long had experimented with ether, a gas that he thought might be useful for putting patients to sleep during surgical procedures. On March 30, 1842, he used sulfuric ether on James Venable, a patient who was having a growth removed from his neck. Venable slept through the entire operation, and Long earned $2 for his services. Today, a monument to Crawford Long sits in the Madison County courthouse in Danielsville.

Aping Human Behavior

Even if we prefer not to admit it, monkeys are a lot like humans, and researchers at the Yerkes National Primate Research Center at Emory University have discovered that monkeys can teach us quite a bit about ourselves. The center was founded by psychobiologist Robert M. Yerkes, PhD, in Florida, but was later relocated to Atlanta. Studying the 3400 monkeys that inhabit the center has helped scientists understand everything from drug addiction to aging and has contributed to the development of an AIDS vaccine.

Two Moos

Moo-ve over Dolly, 'cause here comes KC. Since Dolly the sheep was cloned in Scotland in 1997, researchers around the world have made a veritable menagerie of animal copies. Scientists at the University of Georgia created their own clone, named KC (after the disco-era KC and the Sunshine Band), in April 2002.

Although cows have been cloned before, KC was the first to come from the cells of a dead cow. Despite fears about animal cloning, KC has done just fine. In 2006, she gave birth to her second calf, Moonshine.

Rich and Fat-Free?

Could a fat-free, yet rich-tasting chocolate milkshake be possible? Food scientist Casimir Akoh of the University of Georgia believes so. He is developing fats made from fish oils and other natural substances that reportedly taste as good as regular fats, but with 45 percent fewer calories and about half as much cholesterol. And unlike olestra (which he also helped develop), the new fats won't have nasty digestive side effects.

WHAT'S UP, DOC?

A Tiny Doctor with a Huge Heart

Decades after the demise of the traditional family doctor, Dr.
Leila Denmark still practiced medicine the old-fashioned way,
dispensing tried and true advice along with her prescriptions.
Her fees were also stuck somewhere in the 1950s—in the 70
years that she practiced, the diminutive doctor rarely charged
patients more than $10 for a visit to the Forsyth County farm-
house that served as her office. Denmark was born in Bulloch
County on February 1, 1898, and in 1928, she became only the
third woman to graduate from the Medical College of Georgia
in Augusta. Despite her folksy manner, Denmark conducted
groundbreaking research on whooping cough in the 1930s and
'40s, and her findings helped lead to the development of the life-
saving pertussis vaccine. When she finally retired in 2001 at age
103, Denmark was the oldest practicing pediatrician in the country. Today, at 108, she still offers medical advice over the phone.

From Patient to Doctor

For David Satcher, getting sick as a child was truly a life-changing
experience. When he was just two years old, Satcher nearly died
from whooping cough. Because the local hospital was out of the
question for the African American Satcher family in segregated
Alabama, the local doctor made a house call, trudging several
miles on his day off to treat young David. That moment solidi-
fied Satcher's career aspirations—he wanted to become a doctor.
Satcher graduated Phi Beta Kappa from Morehouse College in
1963. He went on to serve as director of the Centers for Disease
Control and Prevention, and was simultaneously Surgeon General
and Assistant Secretary for Health under President Clinton. In
2001, he was awarded the Jimmy and Rosalynn Carter Award for
Humanitarian Contributions to the Health of Humankind from
the National Foundation for Infectious Disease.

LIFE IN GEORGIA

Hungry?

Georgia is home to 14,843 restaurants. Every food type is represented, from classic Southern cuisine to international ethnic delicacies. But before you order, you should know a few things about the food:

☞ People in Georgia order their tea pre-sweetened, as in, "I'll have a sweet tea."

☞ Macaroni and cheese is considered a vegetable.

☞ If you order greens, you won't get a salad—you'll get a plate of collard, mustard or turnip greens.

☞ A Coke is any type of carbonated soft drink, not just Coca-Cola.

☞ If you have a hankering for barbecue, what you're most likely to get is grilled or smoked pork with a sauce made from vinegar, tomatoes, mustard, sugar and spices. It's served with a thick slice of white bread, along with corn on the cob, baked beans, coleslaw or Brunswick stew (a thick, rich concoction made from meat, onions, lima beans and tomatoes).

☞ Boiled peanuts (pronounced "bahld peanuts" by real Southerners) are a staple of just about every roadside farm stand in Georgia, and a Southern institution since about the time of the Civil War. To make them, you take green (raw) peanuts and boil them in a vat of salty water for about two to four hours, until they're soft inside. Accompany them with a cold beer and you've got the perfect snack.

How to Speak Georgian

Although almost 90 percent of people in Georgia speak English as their primary language, there is a local lingo, and it can leave visitors asking, "What did y'all say?" Here are a few important words and phrases to know:

Phrase: Y'all (short for "you all")
What it means: All of you
Use: "What would y'all like to order?"

Phrase: Fixin' to
What it means: I'm getting ready to do something
Use: "I'm fixin' to mop the floor as soon as I finish scrubbin' the sink."

Phrase: The ATL
What it means: Atlanta
Use: "We're partying in the ATL tonight!"

Phrase: I like to
What it means: I almost had
Use: "I like to had a heart attack."

Phrase: I might could
What it means: I might be able to
Use: "I might could paint that house, if it would stop raining."

OUT AND ABOUT

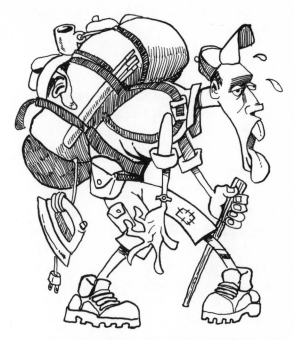

Shooting the Hooch

"Shooting the hooch" in Georgia is not, as it sounds, a reference to blowing away a bottle of illegal liquor. It refers to rafting, canoeing, kayaking or tubing down the 48 miles of the Chattahoochee River National Recreation Area, activities that are a staple of family outings and company picnics in the Atlanta area. The river is also a good place to fish, though the chilly temps (the river stays a numbing 50°F all year) and the occasional broken bottle make the river unsuitable for swimming.

Take a Hike!
With mild temperatures prevailing year round, Georgia is the perfect place to get out and explore nature. Hiking is one activity locals never tire of, and there are many trails from which to choose, including the Appalachian Trail, Amicalola State Park

(which leads to Amicalola State Falls, the tallest cascading waterfall in the southeast) and the Bartram Trail (on which hikers can follow in the footsteps of 18th-century naturalist William Bartram).

Concerts

Just about every touring rock band, country act, theater troupe and comedian around the country passes through Georgia at some point. Depending on their popularity, acts can play at one of the huge stadiums or small, intimate theaters scattered throughout Atlanta and other parts of the state. Here are just a few of the many places in Georgia to catch a show:

☛ The Fox Theatre. When seeing a show at the Fox, it's best to come early, because the theater is as much a part of the show as the actual performance. Originally built as a Yaarab Temple Shrine Mosque, the Fox looks like the inside of an Arab courtyard, complete with minarets and faux twinkling stars in the sky. When it opened in 1929, the Fox was the grand dame of movie houses. Even though the era of movie palaces is long gone, the theater has made a tradition of its summer movie series. Each movie kicks off with a sing-along with the "Mighty Mo," a 4000-pipe theatrical organ that has been in existence since the theater opened.

☛ Atlanta Civic Center. The largest theater in the southeast, and the home of the Atlanta Opera, the center can comfortably seat 4600. It's also a great place to catch ballet, theater and concerts.

☛ Phillips Arena. When the Police reunited after 20 years for one of the most highly anticipated tours of 2007, they came to Phillips Arena. Keith Urban, Justin Timberlake, Billy Joel and Rod Stewart have also played this $213 million mega-arena, which can hold up to 21,000 screaming fans. Sports are another big attraction at Phillips—the venue is home to the Hawks, Thrashers and the Georgia Force.

☛ Chastain Park. Tucked in a tree-lined Atlanta suburb is a venue where it's become a summertime tradition to picnic under the stars while listening to amazing music. Watching a concert at Chastain Park is more than a show—it's an all-night dinner-and-dancing event. When the lights go down, the candelabras light up the tables, which are covered in a colorful assortment of entrees and decked out in fine china and fancy stemware. Many of the acts will make you nostalgic for your bellbottoms and roller skates (think KC and the Sunshine Band and REO Speedwagon). Outside the perimeter are two cozier versions of Chastain Park that have their own summertime concert series. Peachtree City has the Frederick Brown Jr. Amphitheater (affectionately nicknamed "The Fred"), and Mableton has the Mable House Arts Center.

☛ Woodruff Arts Center. Built with a generous grant from former Coca-Cola president Robert Woodruff, this is the center for visual and performing arts in Atlanta. Within its complex are the Alliance Theatre, High Museum of Art, Atlanta Symphony Orchestra, and 14th Street Playhouse.

☛ Hugh Hodgson Concert Hall. It may be situated on a university campus (the University of Georgia, to be exact), but this performing arts center has all the makings of a top-notch concert hall. In fact, some people think its acoustics are the best in the state. The Atlanta Symphony makes regular appearances here, as do music and dance acts from around the world.

Cha-Ching!

Shopaholics rejoice—Georgia is chock-full of stores where locals and visitors can flex their purchasing muscles. From the upscale boutiques of Buckhead to the bargain-filled outlet malls, there is something for every budget. Here's a quick window-shop of the top stores in the state:

☛ Phipps Plaza. Nothing less than the most upscale shops would do for a mall in the heart of swanky Buckhead. Stroll through this shopper's paradise and you'll pass more than 100 designer boutiques, including Jimmy Choo, Giorgio Armani and Gucci.

☛ The Mall of Georgia. Although it isn't the biggest mall in the country (Mall of America in Minnesota has that distinction), the Mall of Georgia in Buford is a major attraction in its own right. It encompasses 2.2 million square feet of pure shopping bliss. In addition to its five department stores and 225 retail shops, the mall has a 500-seat amphitheater, Vans Skatepark, NASCAR racing simulation and a 20-screen movie theater with its own IMAX theater. Each massive section of the mall is named for one of the five natural regions in the state: Mountain, Piedmont, Atlanta, Plains and Coastal.

☛ North Georgia Premium Outlets. All over northern Georgia you can hear the exclamation, "You got that outfit for *how much*?" That's because the North Georgia Premium Outlets in Dawsonville have some of the best bargains in the state. Shoppers can save anywhere from 25 to 65 percent at high-end retailers such as Calvin Klein, Kenneth Cole, Hugo Boss, Williams-Sonoma, Crabtree & Evelyn and about 135 other stores.

☛ Virginia Highlands. At the intersection of Virginia and Highland Avenues is an eclectic, artsy neighborhood packed with art galleries, antique stores, coffeehouses and funky clothing boutiques.

Fore!

Georgia is a golfer's dream come true. The state is home to so many courses that you could play a different one almost every day of the year. The Savannah Golf Club has been around longer than any other course in the country. Georgia also hosts the most prestigious golf tournament, The Masters, at the Augusta National Golf Club.

DID YOU KNOW?

Jack Nicklaus was the all-time leader in Masters wins, with victories in 1963, 1965, 1966, 1972, 1975 and 1986. In 1997, Tiger Woods became the youngest Masters champion—he was just 21 years old.

In 2003, Martha Burk, head of the National Council of Women's Organizations, stirred things up at the normally staid club when she protested Augusta's policy of excluding women from its membership. As the demonstrations heated up and advertisers began to waffle, organizers decided to run the event commercial free, a move that cost the club an estimated $7 million.

ANNUAL TRADITIONS

March with Pride

Atlanta has long been known as a gay-friendly city. That's not surprising, considering that it has the third highest gay population in the country—almost 40,000 residents. Every spring, the city hosts one of the biggest gay events in the Southeast—the Gay Pride Festival and Parade. About 300,000 gay, lesbian, bisexual and transgender people come to town to hear music, listen to speakers and take part in the colorful parade of floats down Peachtree Street. The African American gay community hosts its own Pride event every Labor Day weekend.

Chili Cook-Off

Every fall, hordes of chili fanatics converge on Stone Mountain to celebrate the spicy mix of meat and beans. In 2007, its 28th year, the festival drew some 300 amateur chili chefs from around the country, all vying for the $4000 top prize. Past winners have included "Trailer Trash Chili" and "Cooter Chili," which undoubtedly taste better than they sound. To make sure visitors don't overdo it on the free chili, the festival has plenty of other activities, such as the Mullet Flop, which challenges racers to make it to the finish line first without dropping a raw fish trapped between their teeth.

Pan African Festival

This weeklong event, held every spring in Macon, pays tribute to African culture, while embracing the spirit of harmony among all peoples. The festival features jazz, reggae and hip-hop music, activities for the kids and a tantalizing array of African American and Caribbean foods.

Sweet Auburn Springfest
Since civil rights leader Hosea Williams founded the Sweet
Auburn Springfest in 1984, it has grown into a huge street party
in downtown Atlanta, and one of the most vibrant celebrations
of African American culture in the southeast. The three-day
event takes place along historic Auburn Avenue, where festi-
val-goers can sample from a variety of foods, listen to live music
on one of seven stages and browse the colorful works on display
in the artists' market. The festival also features an Arts and
Literature Market, Business and Technology Expo and the
Sweet Auburn International Film Festival.

St. Patty's Day in Savannah

Although Savannah isn't the first place most people would think
of in connection with Irish culture, it actually hosts one of the
biggest and wildest St. Patty's Day celebrations in the country.
Its parade is second only to New York in size, with nearly half
a million people packing the streets and waterfront. For the day,
everything is green in Savannah—the food, the beer and even
the fountains.

Steeplechase

The annual Atlanta Steeplechase, held in Rome, is as much a
"see and be seen" social gathering as it is a sporting event.
Young socialites come in their finest party dresses and sun hats
to watch thoroughbreds vie for a purse estimated at more than
$150,000. The luckiest visitors get to party in one of the posh
corporate tents. The event isn't all about excess, though—it's
actually a party with a purpose, raising money for the
University of Georgia College of Veterinary Medicine and the
Starlight Starbright Children's Foundation.

Peachtree Road Race

Every July 4th, more than 50,000 runners line up in Buckhead's Lenox Square at 7:30 AM, waiting in the steamy summer heat for the start of the annual Peachtree Road Race, the nation's largest 10K event. The race is so big that it takes more than an hour from the official start for the last runner to make it past the starting line. From there it's a demanding 6.5 mile-run, often uphill, along the city's main thoroughfare all the way to Piedmont Park in Midtown. Why do they do it? The top runners can nab a purse upwards of $10,000, but anyone who finishes below the top 20 has to settle for a T-shirt and a sense of accomplishment.

DID YOU KNOW?

Collectively, the 50,000 or so runners of the Peachtree Road Race drink 120,000 gallons of water and burn *34 million* calories.

Blessing of the Fleet

The Blessing of the Fleet comes from Portuguese tradition, in which Catholic priests in fishing villages would give their blessings as boats left, to ensure a bountiful fishing season. Two towns in coastal Georgia, Darien and Brunswick, have picked up on this tradition and celebrate it each year. In Darien, highlights of the event include the Little Miss Blessing of the Fleet Pageant, a tricycle race and a street parade. In both towns, the shrimp boats get decked out for the occasion, and a member of the local clergy blesses each one as it passes.

DRUGS, BOOZE AND ALL THINGS NAUGHTY

Drink Up!

Back in 1907, most Georgia counties were dry. Still, bootleggers were making a bundle selling the contraband. Today's liquor laws are far more relaxed, though some counties in rural areas remain booze free. Even in counties where liquor is allowed, buying it on Sunday is a big no-no (though lawmakers and liquor lobbyists are trying to change the "blue laws"). You can order a drink in a restaurant on Sunday, but you have to wait until 12:30 PM.

Drug Busts

Law enforcement officials say that drugs are big business in Georgia thanks to readily accessible interstates that provide speedy drug traffic distribution routes from Mexico. Here are just a few of the big busts that have been made in the state:

- ☛ October 2005: Federal agents arrested 28 people and nabbed 1300 pounds of cocaine and $8 million, breaking up one of the biggest drug rings on the East Coast.

- ☛ August 2006: Police in Gainesville seized 341 pounds of methamphetamine, worth an estimated $50 million.

- ☛ April 2007: A routine traffic stop led Forsyth County police to discover three suitcases filled with cocaine—a whopping 132 pounds worth an estimated $4 million.

With drug trafficking heating up, police have been on the hunt for suspects. One of those investigations turned tragic in November 2006, when Atlanta narcotics officers serving a warrant shot and killed 92-year-old Kathryn Johnston in her home after she reportedly fired shots at them. It turned out the officers were at the wrong house. The botched raid led police to start scrutinizing the "no-knock raids" that led to Johnston's death.

Adult Entertainment

For a state that's smack dab in the middle of the Bible Belt, Georgia has plenty of places for people to get nasty. Besides the dozens of strip clubs, there are swinger's clubs (Club 2 Risque and Club Venus), gay/lesbian clubs (Swinging Richards, Girls in the Night) and adult entertainment stores (Inserection, Love Shack and Starship Enterprises) galore.

Gold Club

It was one of the hottest clubs in the country, hosting elite athletes such as Dennis Rodman and Patrick Ewing. But then came the news in 2001 that the strippers were performing more than just dances for their celebrity clientele. Before the sentences were handed out, Gold Club owner Steve Kaplan cut a $5 million plea deal to reduce his prison term, and now the Gold Club is no more. But don't despair, gentlemen: Georgia has plenty of other places to see the lovely ladies, including the Cheetah Club, the Pink Pony and the Oasis Good Time Emporium.

OFF THE BEATEN PATH

Market House

Some sources date the building of the old Market House in Louisville to sometime between 1758 and 1790, making it the oldest structure of its kind in the city—erected, in fact, before the city was even founded. Folks flocked there to purchase their weekly food supplies, and although there is much dispute to the claim, Market House was also thought to be home to the slave trade.

Musician Memorialized

Although his life was cut down in its prime by a tragic airplane crash, Otis Redding's memory lives on. In homage to his most popular song, a seven-foot-tall bronze statue of the soul singer sits on a dock in Macon's Gateway Park, strumming a guitar. The town raised more than $50,000 to build the statue in order to honor the man whose music they say brought people together.

The Real Thing

Atlanta's new World of Coca-Cola, opened in May 2007, is a shrine to the bubbly stuff, and a must-see for Coke enthusiasts. Covering an area of more than 62,000 square feet, the new World of Coca-Cola is about double the size of its previous incarnation and equally as self-promotional. Visitors can walk through the soda's 120-year history, watch a 3-D movie and peruse exhibition halls filled with the largest collection of Coke memorabilia on the planet. Along with 50 exhibits from the previous museum, another 1200 artifacts collected from around the world are on display. At the end of the tour, guests get to sample any of 70 different soda flavors from around the world.

Biggest and Best

To say the peanut is revered in Georgia is a bit of an understatement. The peanut has been the official crop since 1995, and if you're driving near Ashburn, try heading off the I-75 for just a few moments and check out what folks in these parts call the "World's Largest Peanut." A peanut shell perched on one end atop a brick tower has been there since it was erected in February 1975, perhaps as a salute to the city's nickname, "Peanut Capital of the World." The small city also once boasted the world's largest peanut-shelling plant.

Set in Stone

No visit to Georgia is complete without a stop at Stone Mountain, a family fun park that pays homage to the state's Civil War history. The centerpiece of Stone Mountain Park is the 825-foot-tall mountain itself, with its giant carving of Confederate legends Jefferson Davis, General Robert E. Lee and Lieutenant General Thomas "Stonewall" Jackson. The idea for the carving came from Helen Plane, the chapter president of what is now known as the United Daughters of the Confederacy. The effort began in 1923, led by artist Gutzon Borglum. Eventually Borglum left the project to work on another well-known carving—Mount Rushmore in South Dakota—and another artist, Augustus Lukeman, took over. Then Lukeman died, and in 1958, the State of Georgia took over the unfinished monument.

Creating the enormous granite carvings was no easy feat, and Stone Mountain wasn't entirely finished until the early 1970s. The entire carving is as wide across as three football fields, and Jackson's nose is 41 feet long—quite a honker. To view the carving up close, visitors can either climb the 1.1-mile trek to the mountain summit, or take the more leisurely Summit Skyride in a Swiss cable car.

Holy Cow!

It appears that paying tribute to the nation's dairy industry is quite common, if you judge by the number of fiberglass cow mascots dotting the countryside. Not to be outdone, Georgia is home to its very own roadside bovine. Kadie the Cow once loomed large, overlooking the I-94 from the hillside of her family farm near Columbus. In 2004, after her farm owners retired, Kadie was moved to a nearby Best Buy store.

Plump and Juicy?

If the country's roadside attractions are any indication, Americans are serious about eating healthy. Giant fiberglass fruit can be spotted along the highways and byways from Winchester to Virginia to Texas and California, and all points in-between. Georgia's famous fruits include the big apple of Cornelia and a peach (of course!) near Byron.

Hop By, Any Time

If you've always dreamed of visiting Australia but never got around to it, why not check out "America's Aussie Adventure." Located in Dawsonville is the Kangaroo Conservation Center, and with more than 300 kangaroos on site at any given time, it has the largest kangaroo herd outside Australia. The center is actually a breeding facility but welcomes visitors to what it calls a "unique wildlife educational adventure." Along with the chance to see as many as a dozen different species of kangaroo, guests to the center can follow a quarter-mile-long hiking trail where they can catch a glimpse of some of this country's most endangered animals, such as the Eastern box turtle. Although the conservation center is fun for the whole family, only children over the age of eight are admitted.

Someone to Love

Human nature being what it is, we all need someone to love, and that someone special could be a favorite friend, relative, beau—or in the case of Calculator, a dog. In actual fact, Calculator was little more than a freeloading mutt, living off the kindness of the military folks stationed at Fort Benning in the 1920s. He was given the moniker "Calculator" because he'd often hobble along on three legs, especially when he was hungry. His "calculating" charade must have worked, because the servicemen there adopted the mangy mutt as their own, housing him in their barracks and enduring his shadow-like presence wherever they went. Someone, however, had a less than favorable view of old Calculator. In 1923, a little something was added to his daily meal—a dose of strychnine. He was laid to rest at the fort, and money was raised for a plaque in his honor, which reads:

Calculator
Born ?
Died Aug. 29, 1923
He Made Better Dogs of Us All

For dog lovers interested in checking out this memorial, the plaque is secured to a rock in the front of the National Infantry Museum.

Furor Over the Fuhrer

It appears that a walking stick, several beer steins, desk keys and other personal items of Hitler's were transported into the country after the war and are now housed in museums across the U.S. Georgia has at least one exhibit once belonging to the notorious despot: an upside-down bronze Hitler head can be found at the National Infantry Museum at Fort Benning.

Front and Center

A marker erected on Highway 29 South, near Hartwell, makes the bold claim of being the "Center of the World." The location was first given the title by Cherokee Natives, who reasoned that it deserved the distinction because several trails met there, and for the Cherokee Nation it certainly served the purpose. In a sense, Hartwell *is* the center of the world for folks in Hart County—it's the county seat.

Lunchbox Heaven

In life, you've really got to keep your eyes open if you want to experience the many gems hidden in obscure places. Such is the case with the Lunchbox Museum in Columbus. Tucked away in a portion of the International Marketplace is what organizers believe to be the world's largest collection of metal lunchboxes. Literally thousands of lunchboxes and other noontime collectibles line the museum shelves, all in pristine condition and bearing colorful caricatures of favorite TV personalities, such as Soupy Sales, Hopalong Cassidy, the Six Million Dollar Man, Wonder Woman and even the entire Walton clan. According to the museum, the metal lunchbox craze—as opposed to the metal pail craze of our pioneering forefathers—kicked into motion around 1951. Plastic replaced metal around 1986.

(Apparently Florida deemed the metal versions "lethal weapons," and the ruling had a widespread effect.) In any case, the era has long passed but is fondly remembered by visitors to this Columbus attraction.

It's a Bird?

Deep-fried chicken lovers won't have to worry about how to find the Kentucky Fried Chicken outlet in Marietta. Towering 56 feet high, an abstract sort of chicken, complete with moveable eyes and beak, overlooks patrons as they visit the fast-food franchise. It's so big that locals use the "Big Chicken" as a sort of landmark to find their way around the Marietta area (as in, "turn left at the Big Chicken"). The story goes that the chicken was erected in 1963 by a fellow named Tubby Davis, who operated a Johnny Reb's Chick, Chuck and Shake outlet. Eventually the business closed shop, and in 1974, KFC leased the building and added its logo to the bird's "wings." A few years later, the franchise wanted to open up another operation in Smyrna, but residents there wanted a similar big chicken mascot, and to satisfy their request, KFC planned to move the Marietta bird. That didn't go over well with residents in Marietta, and after they sounded their concerns loud and clear, the bird stayed put.

My Lady

Bet you didn't know Georgia had its very own Statue of Liberty.
To honor the 100th anniversary of the statue in 1986, the Lions
Club in McRae took it upon itself to create a replica at one-
twelfth of the original size. With a city population of 2682, the
club wasn't exactly overrun with members possessing a large
bank account. So to successfully complete the task, they had to
make do with whatever materials they could scrounge up
around town—Styrofoam, a tree stump, an electrician's glove
and so on. The end result is a mighty fine likeness of our Lady
Liberty, front and center in McRae's Liberty Square, alongside
a replica of the Liberty Bell. Talk about patriotic!

Wascally Wabbit

It's probably only fitting for a place called Rabbittown to have
a giant statue in honor of its namesake. The 20-foot-tall bunny
sits in a parking lot on Old Cornelia Road, one paw raised in
a friendly wave. Since the statue was built in 1993, tourists have
come from all over to have their pictures taken with the was-
cally wabbit.

Big Red

Cornelia is known for its big, red roadside attraction—and it's
not Clifford, the children's cartoon dog. In a tribute to the
county's apple growers, a steel and concrete statue measuring
seven feet in height, 22 feet in circumference and weighing
5200 pounds was built in 1925 and placed on a pedestal that
states "Home of the Big Red Apple, Habersham County." The
apple industry took hold in the area after World War I, when
farmers discovered that drought, the boll weevil and other
natural pests of the area didn't affect apple trees like they did the
cotton crops. Today there are about 360,000 apple trees in the
state. To commemorate the industry even further, Cornelia hosts
the annual Big Red Apple Festival the first Saturday in October.

Lighting the Way

Cockspur Lighthouse, located on the eastern end of Cockspur Island, was originally erected on an oyster and mussel bed in 1849, but the structure standing today replaced the first one in 1857. Built of brick, the 46-foot tower fared better than its twin tower built on Oyster Bed Island. That structure was destroyed by frequent storms. Cockspur Lighthouse, which is now part of the Fort Pulaski National Monument, ceased active duty in 1909. It is now maintained by the National Park Service. Visitors can learn about the colorful history of the lighthouse and hear seafaring stories and Civil War tales at the Fort Pulaski Visitor's Center.

Set Your Clocks

Everyone in Rome, Georgia, is synchronized, at least as far as their clocks and watches are concerned. Residents of this fine city mark their minutes according to Rome's famous Clock Tower, which overlooks the downtown center. Built in 1871, the 100-foot tower was originally created as Rome's water tower, but in 1872 a massive four-faced clock face was added. With a 9-foot diameter face, a minute hand that measures 4 feet 3 inches, and an hour hand that measures 3 feet 6 inches, the clock allows folks from any vantage point in the city to tell the time just by turning toward Neely Hill.

R.I.P.

Historic Cemetery

If you're into strolling cemeteries to get a glimpse of an area's history, the Oakland Cemetery in Atlanta should be a prime stop on your tour. As the first city cemetery in the area, Oakland Cemetery holds the remains of Confederate soldiers and other noteworthy residents from all walks of life. Among some of the more recognizable names are Margaret Mitchell, author of *Gone With the Wind*; Dr. Joe Jacobs, inventor of Coca-Cola; Morris Rich, founder of Rich's Department Stores; and Wesley John Gaines, a bishop of the African Methodist Episcopal Church.

Young Heroines

Resaca Cemetery in Resaca is certainly worth a visit, especially if you're into Civil War history. Considering that Resaca is the final resting place of more than 400 soldiers, a stroll inside the stone-walled graveyard can't help but take you back in time. But the cemetery is famous for another reason, too. According to legend, Mary Green and her younger sister discovered the bodies of Confederate soldiers and sought to give them a proper burial. Their father, Colonel John Green, supplied them with 2.5 acres of land, and the young women raised money for the project by canvassing friends and acquaintances across Georgia. And so, on October 25, 1866, the first Confederate cemetery in the state was dedicated.

Honoring the Unknown Soldiers

Another historic graveyard is Patrick R. Cleburne Confederate Cemetery, located just outside of town on McDonough Road in Jonesboro. Named for the Confederate general of the same name, the cemetery serves as a final resting place for more than 600 soldiers who perished during the battle of Jonesboro in

1864, as well as several hundred other Confederate soldiers. A monument in the cemetery bears this dedication: "To the Honored Memory of the Several Hundred Unknown Confederate Soldiers…" The cemetery is now maintained by the United Daughters of the Confederacy.

Stonepile Gap

Speaking of graves, there's a pile of rocks just north of Dahlonega at the intersection of U.S. 19 and S.R. 60 that, to all outward appearances, doesn't really look like much. But don't let looks deceive you. The legend goes that the rocks mark the burial ground of a Cherokee named Trahlyta, who as a young woman lived in the neighboring mountains. Depending on who tells the story, either a mountain medicine man or the witch of Cedar Mountain instructed Trahlyta to drink daily from the spring to stay strong and maintain her youth. This she did until she was kidnapped by Wahsega, a Cherokee warrior whom she'd rejected. Saddened by her plight and without her daily drink, Trahlyta became ill and died. Her last request was that Wahsega bury her near her beloved mountain. The historical marker near her grave explains how she promised that those who drop a stone on her grave would be granted good fortune. It is a practice that many tourists follow today.

TOURIST ATTRACTIONS

Let Your Light Shine

The story behind the St. Simons Lighthouse began in 1804, when St. Simons' landowner John Couper deeded four acres of his land to the government for the building of the seaside structure. By 1810, the 85-foot-tall lighthouse was ready to scan the seas, with keeper James Gould working the helm for a princely salary of $400 a year. Gould stayed on at the job until he retired in 1837. By 1862, Confederate soldiers had destroyed that first structure, but 10 years later the government ordered another, larger structure be built in its place. The tower of the second version measured 104 feet, requiring 129 steps on the accompanying iron spiral staircase.

By 1953, lighthouses around the country were all automated, and instead of housing keepers, they were used as offices for various agencies—in this case the Bureau of Commercial Fisheries, Department of the Interior, Fish and Wildlife Service. Today, the lighthouse continues to warn sailors of the dangerous rocky shorelines, but since 2004 it's been owned and cared for by the Coastal Georgia Historical Society.

DID YOU KNOW?

In March 1880, St. Simons Lighthouse keeper Frederick Osborne and his assistant had an argument, in which Osborne was shot dead. After 1880, people reported hearing unexplained footsteps in the tower. Is Osborne's ghost haunting the St. Simons Lighthouse? No one knows for sure, but it lends the place an aura of mystery.

Famed Fort

Georgia is indisputably a great place for history buffs to visit. Fort Hawkins, in the city of Macon, is just one of the state's historic forts. Established in 1806, the fort was initially used as a trading and meeting place for army officials and Native Americans. A clear view to the south and west from the fort's turret also provided settlers of the day with a little added security.

Fort Hawkins was decommissioned in 1828, but the government was immediately petitioned to maintain the site for its historic value. Although the current structure isn't the original, the efforts of those raised voices weren't in vain. A reconstructed Fort Hawkins, exact to the detail, was built on the original site.

Old Fort Jackson

In 1808, the U.S. government purchased Old Fort Jackson in Thunderbolt, which is now part of Savannah. It was named for Revolutionary War soldier James Jackson. The brick structure replaced an earlier earthen fort, which was built in 1776, and is considered the oldest standing fort in Georgia. General William T. Sherman and his troops captured the fort on December 17, 1864, and by 1905 it had been decommissioned. Today it is maintained by the Coastal Heritage Society and is named a National Historic Landmark.

Another Man's Treasure

A small, four-acre section of reclaimed swampland near Summerville has served as a piece of paradise to thousands of visitors over the years. Known as Paradise Gardens, the site blends the natural beauty of the Georgian countryside with art produced by one of the country's most notable folk artists, Reverend Howard Finster. Born in 1917, Finster was already a well-established itinerant preacher by the age of 16, spreading the Gospel message at tent revival meetings across the state. In 1961, Finster started transforming the swampland around his home into a tranquil garden. But in 1976 he believed he'd received a vision from God to create sacred art, which he incorporated into his existing gardens. Using mostly recycled and discarded items such as scrap wood and metal, old jewelry, mirrors, bathtubs and sinks and any other discarded objects, Finster created a world where everything had a specific meaning. By combining biblical messages with his art, he believed he could continue preaching long after he passed away, which occurred in 2001. According to the many people who've visited Paradise Gardens over the years, Finster achieved his goal.

 Among the notable artwork of Reverend Howard Finster is a Coke bottle painting, which is prominently exhibited at the World of Coca-Cola in Atlanta. He also designed album covers for the rock groups REM and Talking Heads and produced the illustrations for the children's book *The Night Before Christmas*.

What'll Ya Have?

Step up to the register at this Atlanta fast-food establishment, and that's the first question you'll hear. Dubbed "the world's largest drive-in restaurant," The Varsity has been serving up burgers, fries and pimento cheese sandwiches since 1928, both in the restaurant and at its drive-in. Although the restaurant began on a modest 70- by 120-foot lot, today the mother location in downtown Atlanta covers two acres and can fit 600 cars and 800 people. Fresh is always best, and a dedication to food made from scratch is what has maintained this roadside restaurant's appeal. Company sources claim "two miles of hot dogs, a ton of onions, 2500 pounds of potatoes, 5000 fried pies and 300 gallons of chili are made from scratch daily," making for a lot of happy customers!

DID YOU KNOW?

Carhops, called "curb men," sing and dance their way to customers at The Varsity Drive-In. Flossy Mae, a loyal employee for more than 50 years, made his mark singing out the menu for customers. And television and movie star Nipsy Russell used to be better known as carhop number 46.

Undersea World

Georgia is home to the world's largest indoor aquarium. Located on Baker Street in downtown Atlanta, the Georgia Aquarium first opened to the public on November 23, 2005. After two years in construction, at a cost of $200 million, the aquarium holds "more than eight million gallons of fresh and marine water and more aquatic life than found in any other aquarium"—roughly 100,000 underwater creatures. Along with getting a look at the live animals, visitors are informed about the undersea world through more than 60 exhibits.

Cultural Icon

If you have a hankering for waffles, there's no better place to go than the Waffle House—at least that's what many folks in Georgia think, since the state is home to the first Waffle House restaurant. The franchise opened for business in Avondale Estates in 1955, the brainchild of Tom Forkner and Joe Rogers Sr. Little did they know that their neighborhood diner would spawn a chain with more than 1500 stores in 25 states across the nation. According to the company's website, since its opening, the Waffle House has served 495,264,367 waffles and almost twice as many cups of coffee. They must be good!

Slave Cabin

An old slave cabin in Eatonton, dubbed the Uncle Remus Museum, welcomes about 12,000 visitors per year. The museum is a salute to Joel Chandler Harris, the writer who penned the series of stories featuring the main character of Uncle Remus. Through him, Harris transcribed many of the folktales he'd heard from plantation slaves and other African Americans. Although some have commended Harris' writings over the years as an effort to preserve African American folklore, others consider him little more than a literary thief. Either way, the museum offers a peek into both the controversial character and life on a southern plantation.

Music Memorabilia

In 1979, Ray Charles became the first musician to be inducted into the Georgia Music Hall of Fame, but 20 years elapsed before an actual building to house the state's music memorabilia was built. The year was 1996, and by then 47 performers and other music icons had already been chosen to stand alongside the jazz and blues master. Located in Macon, the exhibit hall holds all types of memorabilia that recount the history of Georgia's contribution to the music world.

Historic House

Even by today's sometimes extravagant standards, an 18,000-square-foot, 24-room and four-story mansion seems decadent. So when the Hay House was built in Macon in 1859, complete with indoor plumbing, it was quite obviously the talk of the town. Built in the Italian Renaissance Revival style, Hay House was the residence of William B. Johnston and his family until

1926, when the home was sold to a local banker named Parks Lee Hays. The Hays family remained in the house until 1962, when it was converted into a museum. In 1977, Hay House, as it came to be known, was donated to the Georgia Trust for Historic Preservation. Today the museum, which doubles as an education and cultural event center, is a main attraction for folks traveling through the city of Macon.

Building a Civilization

Efforts to build a community in the Macon area date back as early as 1000 BC, when Native Americans built the first great earthen mounds. Although early European settlers to the area destroyed some of the mounds to make way for development, the desire to preserve the remnants of Macon's earliest civilization led to the creation of the Ocmulgee Indian Mounds National Park. Visitors to the site can still view the Great Temple Mound, which measures 50 feet tall on the side that would have faced the village, and 90 feet high on the back side, which flows down to the floodplain. This mound, as well as the Lesser Temple Mound located just a few feet away, both served as platforms or foundations for rectangular-shaped buildings that were likely used for ceremonies and other official village business. A plaque commemorates the Funeral Mound, much of which was destroyed in 1874 during the building of the railroad. The excavation at that time recovered more than 100 remains, along with personal items. Although smaller in scale, four other mounds—Southeast Mound, McDougal Mound, Dunlap Mound and Mound X—are accessible via a walking trail.

Railroad History

There are good reasons why the Southeastern Railroad Museum in Duluth was named the state's official transportation history museum. With more than 90 pieces of rolling stock, it has been open for viewing on the 30-acre site since 1970. Among the amazing displays is a 1911 Pullman private car, a Savannah & Atlanta 4-6-2 Light Pacific steam locomotive, freight cars, cabooses and an assortment of other railroad paraphernalia. Visitors can even ride in an authentically restored caboose pulled by a steam or diesel locomotive.

A-Maize-ing

If your youngsters are among those who think brown cows produce brown milk, or worse still, that milk of any kind comes from the grocery store, then a trip to Cagle's Dairy is likely something to add to your list of things to do. Located near Canton in Cherokee County, Cagle's Dairy calls itself

"An Educational Resource Farm" that specializes in farm tours for schoolchildren. The site has been home to a dairy business since 1923, but the Cagle family took it over in 1951, and today Cagle's Dairy offers school and public tours that include everything from hay rides and herding demonstrations, to the care and feeding of baby calves to the milking of cows. In the fall, visitors can pick pumpkins or get lost in all the twists and turns of Cagle's famous Cornfield MAiZE. It takes about 45 minutes to get through if you don't become hopelessly lost, but be warned—at night all sorts of ghosts and goblins come out to haunt the MAiZE.

Under the Cabbage Patch

Step aside Dr. Spock. In the world of Babyland General Hospital, after a full 10-leaf dilation, babies really do emerge from under the cabbage patch—and more than 250,000 visitors crowd around to applaud the event each year. The makeshift hospital, located in what was once the Neal Clinic in Cleveland, was established in 1979 as the birthplace of Cabbage Patch Kids toys. Visitors are directed to the delivery room by Colonel Casey, the resident stork. Along with a father's waiting room and a delivery room is a nursery where newly delivered Cabbage Patch babies rest and preemies are kept inside incubators. "Healthcare providers" are on hand should the need arise for medical intervention, but visitors are told not to fret since "all surgeries at Babyland are minor and pain free…because we administer generous doses of TLC—Tender Loving Care." Of course, older Cabbage Patch Kids go to Babyland Elementary school and learn everything there is to know about two major fevers to hit the area: "gold fever in 1828 and Cabbage Patch fever in 1983." And certified adoption agents are always on hand looking for new families. So the next time you are in the neighborhood, check out Babyland General. Who knows, you might just walk away with an addition to your family!

Kaleidoscope of Color

A seven-acre site just six miles outside of Buena Vista is home to Pasaquan—an artificial sanctuary of sorts designed and initially maintained by Eddie Owens Martin. To say that Eddie, or St. EOM as he has come to be known, was a bit of an eccentric is an understatement. Born in 1908 to hard-working cotton and sugarcane sharecroppers, Eddie's early days were largely influenced by a stern and somewhat abusive father. By the age of 14 he'd struck out on his own, traveling to New York and studying art while supporting himself with his fortune-telling skills. But in the late 1930s, after a feverish illness, Eddie experienced a vision in which he was visited by futuristic entities from another dimension called "Pasaquan." They'd come to recruit Eddie as a prophet of sorts on earth, and he was told to return to Georgia and set up an earthly Pasaquan—which is exactly what he did. For the remainder of his life he carved out a sanctuary on his family homestead in his own unique and flamboyant style, building pillars and painting brilliantly colored murals, most of which depicted the images of the Pasaquans who'd come to visit him. St. EOM welcomed visitors to his home, continued to tell fortunes and shared his unique perspective of the world as he was directed by his visions. In his last years, St. EOM suffered from heart disease and, unwilling to watch his body deteriorate, he opted to end his own life. For a time the sanctuary he'd so lovingly built fell into ruin. In March 1990, the Marion County Historical Society got involved in preserving the site. Two years later, the Pasaquan Preservation Society was formed, and since 2003 it has been the sole owner of the property.

Long Distance Communication

What would we do without the telephone? The thought is beyond comprehension for us today, but not so long ago the telephone was little more than a novelty that some people thought would never last. But last it did, and the Georgia Rural

Telephone Museum in Leslie boasts the "largest collection of antique telephones and telephone memorabilia in the world," documenting the development of the communication medium from 1876 to today's current wireless options. The museum is housed in an old cotton warehouse from the 1920s.

Two for One

Folks interested in Civil War history and curious about the Great Locomotive Chase can have all their questions answered at the Southern Museum of Civil War and Locomotive History in Kennesaw. Along with detailed information on the lives of Civil War soldiers, visitors learn how locomotives were made in the early 20th century and get a play-by-play of the Civil War's Great Locomotive Chase.

Nature's Masterpiece

If you're into all things nature, few sites can compare with Rock City Gardens. Located on Lookout Mountain, just a stone's throw from the Tennessee border, the now famous gardens got off to a rocky start when it first opened its doors on May 21, 1932. Garnet Carter was the clever entrepreneur who first developed a neighborhood in the coveted area of Lookout Mountain. He painstakingly marked out the 4100 feet of nature trail winding its way through the 700 acres surrounding Rock City and ending at Lover's Leap. His wife, Frieda, transplanted wildflowers along the trail and strategically placed garden statues and gnomes representing fairytale characters, creating a unique rock garden for the public to enjoy. But the location was off the beaten path and not easy to find. To rectify the problem, Garnet launched an advertising campaign like no other of its day, commissioning a sign painter named Clark Byers to paint the sides of barns with the white-lettered words, "See Rock City." Barns from Michigan to Texas were painted with the advertisements, and by the end of the decade the site was well on its way to becoming the national icon it is today. Aside from the majestic trail, Rock City Gardens has a 90-foot waterfall, a 180-foot-long suspension bridge and a clear view of seven states from its Lover's Leap.

That Thar's Gold!
America's first official gold rush took place in White County, Georgia, in 1929, and if you're looking for proof to the claim, just check out the Dahlonega Gold Museum. The story goes that a slave belonging to a man named Frank Logan found a nugget in Duke's Creek that year. The find led to the discovery of two gold belts: the Hall County belt and Rabun County belt. Of the two, the Rabun County belt drew larger numbers of men and machinery to the area. Today the Dahlonega Gold Museum is a National Historic Site and panning for gold is still something visitors like to try their hand at—just for fun, of course.

Southern Charm

Who hasn't heard of *Gone With the Wind?* The book, written in 1929 and published in 1936, catapulted its author, Margaret Mitchell, into the public spotlight and international fame. Within a year of its printing, it was nominated for and won a Pulitzer Prize. After that success, Mitchell sold the movie rights to David O. Selznick, and on December 15, 1939, *Gone With the Wind* captivated a nation as it opened in theaters across the U.S. Today the Margaret Mitchell House, the Atlanta home where Margaret and her husband rented a room, has been converted into a museum. Although the house fell victim to several fires, it was meticulously renovated each time. Visitors can tour exhibits recounting the story of Mitchell's life and illustrating the journey of *Gone With the Wind* from book to movie.

Tarleton Oaks

Another tribute to old Tara is the Tarleton Oaks and the Gone
With the Wind Hall of Stars Museum, a bed and breakfast
based on the movie. Along with displays of rare photographs
and other movie memorabilia, the museum treats visitors to a
unique hour-and-a-half-long tour of the museum and its exhibits. In 2000, Fred and Terry Crane bought the plantation-style
home, which was originally built in Barnesville in 1859. (In the
movie, Fred played Brent Tarleton, one of Scarlett's ardent suit-
ors.) Not only is the site a must-see for *Gone With the Wind*
fans, but it also will intrigue followers of the paranormal. Some
visitors have reported seeing ghostly images of a Confederate
soldier and a woman in black and have heard three children
playing in the attic, only to find that no one was there.

Mighty Fighters

A more recent memorial to wartime heroics can be found at the
Mighty Eighth Air Force Museum in Pooler. The National
Guard Armory in Savannah was once home to the Eighth Air
Force. Put into action on January 28, 1942, less than two months
after the nation was shocked by the attack on Pearl Harbor, the
Eighth Air Force would prove to be the "greatest air armada in
history," conducting aerial attacks against Nazi-occupied Europe.
The idea of establishing a museum to honor the more than
350,000 members of the Eighth Air Force, many of whom were
killed in action or became prisoners of war, was the brainchild of
Major General Lewis E. Lyle. In 1983, Lyle, along with other
World War II veterans, began making plans for the museum, and
on May 14, 1996, the 90,000-square-foot Mighty Eighth Air
Force Museum was dedicated and opened to the public. The
museum is divided into galleries that take visitors on a journey
through the events leading up to World War II and beyond.
A number of combat planes have been restored and are on display
in the combat gallery. Another gallery provides a look at what life
might have been like for prisoners of war, and still another exam-
ines the plight of European minorities against Nazi forces.

Battleground Memories

The Chickamauga and Chattanooga National Military Park is the oldest park of its kind in the country. Created in 1890, the park was designed to preserve the historic battlefields where Union and Confederate soldiers battled over control of Chattanooga. At the time, Chattanooga was considered to be the gateway to the South. The park, located just outside of Fort Oglethorpe, offers visitors a seven-mile self-guided auto tour. Memorials and tablets along the way provide historic information, and a visitor center contains additional exhibits, as well as a 26-minute multimedia presentation of the Battle of Chickamauga. During the busy summer tourist season, the park sometimes holds live demonstrations, giving visitors an even clearer picture of what a soldier's life was like in the nation's early days.

If These Walls Could Talk

Folks visiting Oconee County won't have to go far to experience a bit of the area's history. Just stop by the Eagle Tavern Museum and Welcome Center, located in Watkinsville right across from the Oconee County Courthouse, and you'll not only get all the free information you'll need for your visit, but you'll also take a walk back in time. Eagle Tavern is believed to be one of the oldest buildings in Oconee County. Built sometime between 1794 and 1801, the tavern is thought to have served a number of purposes: a protective fort, an inn and tavern and a stagecoach stop. The building is full of historic furnishings and paraphernalia, including an original loom, old liquor bottles and even utensils made from bone, and staff are dressed in period costume.

SMALL TOWN ODDITIES

Swamp Gravy

It's simple to make the down-home recipe of swamp gravy—toss a few potatoes, onions and assorted extras into fish drippings, thicken and serve the stew-type dish nice and warm. It's this "little bit of this and little bit of that" mentality that produced *Swamp Gravy,* which was made the Official Folk Life Play of Georgia in 1994. Patrons at *Swamp Gravy's* seasonal performances in Colquitt are promised an experience "that united a town and moved a nation." The play, which is performed in a renovated 70-year-old cotton warehouse, tells the stories of the community in an effort to preserve Colquitt's rich history. The idea took form in 1991, and stories originally collected and recorded by volunteers were developed into plays set to music. The goal of the process was to retell Southern life the way it was, and is, today.

Colquitt is the "Mayhaw Capital of the World." To celebrate the tart fruit, which is a member of the rose family and a favorite of jelly makers in the area, the annual National Mayhaw Festival is held the third weekend in April.

Pretty in Pink

Macon calls itself the "Cherry Blossom Capital of the World." With more than 275,000 Yoshino cherry trees in the city, is it any wonder?

Proud and Patriotic

There weren't a lot of folks in Wellston in the 1930s. Back then, the town described itself as "a mere train stop located in the middle of a large dairy farm." But small is sometimes mighty, and the community wound up beating out Atlanta as the site of a proposed military air force base. Construction on the $10 million project began in 1941, but when it came to naming the facility, there was a bit of a problem. Colonel Thomas, the base's first commander, wanted to name it after his mentor, Brigadier General Augustine Warner Robins. But army protocol dictated that a new facility must be named after the community supporting it. The city government, however, was so appreciative to be chosen as the site for the base that they voted to change its name. Hence, "Wellston" became "Warner Robins," and the neighboring base was named Robins Field. In 1948, it was renamed Robins Air Force Base.

Honoring the Dead

The coasts of St. Simons Island are truly beautiful, but sadly, many sailors lost their lives in the sea that breaks along its shores. Sculptor Keith Jennings was commissioned to create a work of art in their honor. Because the downed ships were built from St. Simons oak trees, Jennings carved the faces of the sailors, and a number of Native faces as well, into the oak trees of the island, creating a living and somewhat eerie canvas. Visitors to St. Simons can view these "Tree Spirits," as they've come to be known, while strolling down the public trail near Redfern Village.

GHOST TOWNS

Andersonville Prison

Located in Sumter County, Andersonville Prison is also known as Camp Sumter. The prison was one of the largest to be erected during the American Civil War. It was built in 1864, and within a year, as many as 13,000 Union prisoners had perished there. The smattering of remaining buildings and stockade has been named a National Historic Site.

Campbellton

Little remains of what was once the county seat of Campbell County. Founded in 1830, the community was once home to a thriving population of more than 1000 people. But it appears those early residents were a tad shortsighted, and when the Atlanta & West Point Railroad started plotting its route, Campbellton residents said they didn't want it running through their town—it would be too noisy. So the railroad passed by Fairburn instead, and by 1870 that community was the county seat. Today, all that remains of Campbellton are a couple of churches and cemeteries, a Masonic lodge, an old house and a few historic markers.

White Sulfur Springs

The few foundation remnants, stairs and lampposts that remain of White Sulfur Springs are now on private property. But the site, north of Gainesville, was once home to a health resort that was founded sometime around 1846. A hotel owned by J.W. Oglesby welcomed visitors to the area until about 1930. Most of his wealth was tied up in the stock market, and when it crashed in 1929, Oglesby could not afford to maintain the hotel. In 1933, the once popular destination burned to the ground.

Fort McAllister

As far as ghost towns go, Fort McAllister is certainly unique—most of the site is underground. Fort McAllister is actually a collection of earthwork fortifications used during the Civil War. Today it's been preserved as a state park near Richmond Hill.

Sweetwater Creek

A trail leads visitors to the remains of the New Manchester Manufacturing Company's textile mill. Most of the mill was destroyed by fire during the Civil War, but some of the three-story brick façade remains. The trail continues along the creek and to the George Sparks Reservoir. The site, located near Atlanta, is now a state park.

STRANGE AND BIG THINGS

America's Stonehenge

Six granite slabs, each measuring about 19 feet in height and weighing 25 tons apiece, stand on a hillside near Nuberg in Elbert County. How the Georgia Guidestones came to be is as much of a mystery today as it was in 1980, when a gentleman with a plan approached the Elberton Granite Association in Nuberg. R.C. Christian (not his real name) provided the following directions: the company was to build a modern-day incarnation of Stonehenge in a nearby field, inscribe the stones to his specifications and use the $50,000 that he'd deposited in a local bank to cover the costs. The mysterious stranger was never heard from again.

The Georgia Guidestones are carved with the "Ten Commandments for the coming Age of Reason" in many languages, including Russian, Hebrew, Swahili, Greek and Egyptian hieroglyphics. Altogether, the monument contains 951 cubic feet of granite and weighs approximately 237,746 pounds.

It's fitting that Elbert County was chosen as the site of this unique monument, since it has long considered itself the "granite capital of the world." To get the most out of a visit to the Georgia Guidestones, check out the Elberton Granite Association's Granite Museum and Exhibit, which features historical granite displays, antique tools and, of course, information on the Georgia Guidestones.

Land of Covered Bridges

Georgia is rife with history, and among the many historic structures preserved throughout the years is an assortment of covered bridges. Sadly, of the more than 250 such structures thought to dot the Georgian countryside in the 1800s and 1900s, only a few still stand. Efforts from neighboring communities and historical societies have refurbished many of those that remain. The Georgia Department of Transportation offers the public an exemplary map of the state's remaining covered bridges, and here's what you might find if you're inclined to check out a few of the sites:

☛ Elder's Mill Covered Bridge near Watkinsville is just a little off the beaten path. Originally located on the Watkinsville-Athens Road when it was built in 1897, the structure was moved to Rose Creek in 1924 when construction began on what is now Highway 441. Because the bridge was in such good condition, the move helped workers access the nearby Elder's Mill. That mill closed in 1941, but the bridge still exists as a remnant of the period's history.

☛ Another bridge initially built to provide easy access to a mill is the Watson Mill Bridge near Comer in Madison County. The massive 236-foot-long bridge was built in 1885, but when it was moved to its present location it was shortened to 229 feet. Still, it is the longest covered bridge in the state and is listed on the National Register of Historic Places. The 1018 acres surrounding it make up the Watson Mill Bridge State Park.

☛ On the other end of the spectrum is Lula Bridge, built in 1915. Located south of the town of Lula, the bridge is on the site of an abandoned golf course. At a scant 34 feet, it is the smallest covered bridge in the state and one of the smallest in the country.

☛ Nestled in Fannie Askew Williams Park, the Coheelee Bridge has the distinction of being the southernmost historic covered bridge in the U.S. It took 36 workers about four months to complete the construction of the 121-foot bridge in 1891.

☛ James M. "Pink" Hunt built the Cromer's Mill Bridge in Franklin County in 1907. The bridge spans Nails Creek and once provided access to a woolen mill, cotton gin, flour mill and sawmill that were all located in the area. The 110-foot bridge underwent renovations in September 1999, which managed to save the structure from its otherwise inevitable demise.

☛ The Red Oak Creek Bridge, located between Gay and Woodbury on SR 85, is the oldest remaining structure of its kind in the state. After some minor repairs in the late 1990s, the bridge was reopened to traffic. At 252.5 feet from the start of one approach to the end of the other, it's actually the longest wooden bridge in Georgia. But because the cover doesn't span the entire expanse, the bridge doesn't surpass Watson Mill Bridge as the longest covered bridge in the state.

☞ Stone Mountain Covered Bridge wasn't originally built to
   provide access to a picnic area, as it does today. Built in 1891,
   the 151-foot-long bridge initially spanned the Oconee River
   in Clarke County. In 1965, at a price of $18,001—a dollar
   for the bridge and $18,000 in moving costs—it took center
   stage at its new location at Stone Mountain Park, where it
   allows visitors to cross to the Indian Island picnic area.

☞ A piece of Georgia history was almost lost in 1994. That's
   the year intense flooding swept away the 102-year-old
   Auchumpkee Creek Bridge. But the Upson County Historic
   Preservation Commission wasn't content to let Mother
   Nature have her way. Thanks to their efforts, along with
   financial assistance from the Federal Emergency
   Management Agency, parts of the bridge were salvaged and
   used to rebuild the bridge in 1997.

☞ A second bridge bearing the name Watson Mill Bridge is
   located in George L. Smith State Park. Built in 1880, the
   bridge is truly unique in that it is a mill and bridge in one.
   The mill portion is powered by the dam underneath, and the
   openings on either side of the structure allow traffic to pass.

☞ If you're passing by the Euharlee Creek Bridge near the town
   of Euharlee, keep your eyes open for the ruins of the old mill
   that once operated there. The bridge was built in 1886, and

you can get a real feel for the area's history in another neighboring structure—the cow-shed-turned-museum.

☛ The Concord Covered Bridge in Cobb County was built in 1872, but it wasn't the first bridge to span the Nickajack Creek. The original bridge was erected in the 1840s, but was destroyed during the Civil War. Just under 132 feet in length, the structure underwent repairs in 1999 and remains in service today.

☛ Built in 1901, the Poole's Mill Bridge in Forsyth County also went through considerable refurbishing to save it from destruction. Local political leaders designated funds to develop a surrounding park, picnic pavilion and horseshoe pits for visitors to enjoy.

☛ The Stovall Mill Bridge was constructed in 1895, but it too replaced an earlier bridge that had been washed away by the flooding of Chickagauga Creek. Its claim to fame was a starring role in the 1951 movie *I'd Climb the Highest Mountain,* starring Susan Hayward.

☛ Built in 1905, the 164-foot Howard's Bridge is located in an isolated spot in Oglethorpe County. It was originally constructed using "convict labor" and was refurbished in 1998.

☛ Although the Rockdale County Bridge that was built in 1997 doesn't have the history of the other covered bridges, its design emulates bridges of the 1800s. It does have a few extra bells and whistles, however, such as hidden cameras, smoke detectors and a sprinkler system—just in case of fire.

BIGGEST, BEST AND MOST UNIQUE

Bowling Brilliance

Age is certainly no barrier for Bill Hargrove of Clermont. On May 16, 2007, at 106 years of age, the avid bowler officially became the world's oldest league bowler. Media gathered to profile the senior at the Suburban Lanes outside Atlanta that day, and although he was quick to point out that he's not as accurate as he used to be, Hargrove still averaged 97 points a game during the 2006–07 league season.

Just outside of Unadilla, a one-of-a-kind community sprang up, overnight it seemed. With little more than a vision and a million dollars, Wayne Smith and his business partner Marvin Jones created Angel City. They officially unveiled it in April 2006, and so far the Western-styled complex geared to motorcyclists has been a hit. The town boasts two saloons that offer beer for $2, a wide array of hunger-satisfying grub and, perhaps most importantly, a place where bikers can gather, camp out and ride together. According to recent reports, Angel City is truly "a biker's paradise."

Purple Power

When Jacob Paulk moved from farming cotton to muscadine grapes in the 1970s, he initially did so because the agriculture industry of the day was changing and he thought he could carve a niche for himself in the fruit market. Little did he know that he'd eventually become instrumental in promoting the antioxidant claims of the fruit and developing it into a number of natural supplements, including a skin powder called Purple Power. Today, Paulk Vineyards claims to be "the largest grower of muscadine grapes in the world."

Living Scripture

Short on Bibles and intent on teaching her students their Sunday school verses, Martha Berry came up with a unique plan. She'd ensure the scriptures were always visible to her students by painting them on the walls of the Possum Tot Church. Built in 1850, the church doubled as a school for area youngsters from 1900 to 1954. The building stands to this day and is lovingly referred to as the "cradle of Berry College." Visitors to the place don't leave without learning that "The eyes of the Lord are in every place beholding the evil and the good."

Artist Haven

One of the oldest art museums in the country, and the oldest in the South, traces its roots back to 1886, when the Telfair family of Savannah opened their home to the public as an art museum and school. The mansion was originally built in 1818–19 for Alexander Telfair and was bequeathed, contents and all, to the Georgia Historical Society in 1875 with the provision that it be used as a museum. An addition, which was built in 1883, featured the Sculpture Gallery and Rotunda, along with the art portion of the museum. Since then, two other buildings were added to the complex: the Owens-Thompson House, donated in 1951, and the Jepson Center for the Arts, which was specifically designed to accommodate traveling exhibitions and was opened in March 2006.

Roll 'Em

Whoever said drive-in theaters were passé? The new Wilderness Outdoor Movie Theater, which is nestled in the foothills by Trenton, opened its gates in 2005 and promises patrons the best seat in the house—in any one of its 500 parking spots. It's been dubbed the world's largest outdoor drive-in movie theater.

A Druid's Paradise

Talk about innovative business ventures. Certified tree climber Genevieve Summers has been dancing with trees her entire life, so founding a company on the practice seemed a natural evolution. Dancing With Trees is based in north Georgia and teaches folks how to climb trees in a way that's safe both for them and the trees. They've taught students as young as four and as old as 81 years. If you can't get to Dancing With Trees, as long as there are trees in your neck of the woods, the class will come to you. The company also offers a unique way to sleep under the stars—suspended between trees.

FAMOUS FIRSTS

Graduation Highlight

Henry O. Flipper was born a slave in Thomasville in 1856. But just 21 years later, in 1877, the young man became the first African American graduate of West Point.

First Female

At the tender age of 13, Georgia-born Gene Cox became the first girl to serve as a page in the U.S. House of Representatives. The year was 1939, and she reportedly earned $4 for a day's work.

Monica Pang is the first woman of Asian American descent to win the title of Miss Georgia. She was awarded the honor in 2006.

Caring for the Homeless

Bethesda Home for Boys in Savannah is one of the oldest orphanages in the country. It first opened its doors in 1742 to care for boys who'd lost their families to war, famine or disease. Construction of the physical building began in 1740 on 500 acres of land and took two years to complete. But the home was plagued with difficulties, including money shortages and two fires. In 1780, a new building was erected. A replica of the George Whitfield Chapel was added in 1925, along with a swimming pool in 2000.

Cool Cola

The first advertisement Coca-Cola painted on the side of a building was on the Young Brothers Pharmacy in downtown Cartersville. The sign made its debut in 1894, reportedly painted by a syrup salesman. It was restored in 1994.

Mighty Fine Music

A first for country music occurred in 1923 when Georgia-born Fiddlin' John Carson recorded the first country music record. John and his daughter, Rosa Lee (Moonshine Kate), were really country music's first stars, and Fiddlin' John's performance of "Little Old Log Cabin in the Lane" was the first country music song broadcast on the radio. The station that helped make music history was WSB in Atlanta.

Home Sweet Home

Most of the developed world has heard of Habitat for Humanity International, especially because former President Jimmy Carter is a very vocal supporter. The nonprofit organization builds houses for people in need, using volunteer labor. But what most people don't know is that the idea for the international organization was born out of the "partnership housing" concept originated by Koinonia Farm, a Christian farming community near Americus.

Household Name

With all of the responsibilities involved with being the wife of a schoolteacher and raising three boys, Caroline Pafford Miller could hardly find time to write. But when she finally put pen to paper, the Baxley resident's words were pure gold. Her first novel, *Lamb in his Bosom*, was published in 1933. The book received critical acclaim and earned Miller the 1934 Pulitzer Prize. She was the first novelist in Georgia to win such an honor.

DID YOU KNOW?

In 1943, Georgia became the first state in the country to allow everyone age 18 and up to vote.

Baseball Highlight

Baseball legend Jackie Robinson was born in Cairo in 1919. He was the first African American to play in the major leagues when he joined the Brooklyn Dodgers in 1947.

Firefighting First

Chief Rosemary Cloud of East Point has the distinction of being the first African American woman to be named fire chief in the entire country. She was appointed to the position in 2002 and is currently in charge of four fire stations and almost 100 firefighters.

Young Blood

Georgia's youngest-ever governor was George Walton. He first took office in 1779 at the tender age of 29. He's also known as one of the youngest men to sign the Declaration of Independence in 1776.

Mineral Discovery

Bauxite, a mineral used in making aluminum, was first discovered in the south of France in 1821. The first North American find of bauxite occurred near Rome in 1887.

THE ART WORLD

Museums

Although the Yanks might condemn the South for its lack of culture, it's actually plentiful in Georgia. The state has more than a dozen different art museums that showcase both local and international collections. Here are a few of the best places in Georgia to view fine art:

☛ Albany Museum of Art. When the museum opened back in 1964, its home was an old hosiery mill. It has been in its current space since 1983 and now has six galleries. In addition to its permanent galleries, which house one of the largest collections of sub-Saharan African art in the Southeast, the museum hosts visiting exhibits from such legendary artists as Norman Rockwell, Edward Hopper and Dorothea Lange.

☛ Brenau University Galleries. When Dr. John S. Burd became president of this Gainesville university in 1985, he realized that the school had a dilemma. There was no place for talented students to display their art. So Burd converted an old chapel into a makeshift art gallery, which today has grown into one of the premiere art collections in the region, with more than 1100 works by artists such as Pierre Auguste Renoir, Paul Cézanne, Eugène Delacroix and Jasper Johns.

☛ Columbus Museum. Outside of Atlanta, one of the best places to learn about the art and history of the region is at the Columbus Museum. The museum celebrates American arts and crafts and lets visitors relive the story of the Chattahoochee River valley from its earliest settlements through the Civil War and into the 20th century.

☛ Georgia Museum of Art. It might surprise visitors to learn that the state's official art museum is not in Atlanta, but in Athens on the campus of the University of Georgia. From its humble beginnings in the basement of an old library on campus, the museum has grown into a 52,000-square-foot exhibit housing 8000 works of art by Georgia O'Keeffe, Childe Hassam, Winslow Homer, Jacob Lawrence and many other American artists. A good portion of the exhibit was donated by the museum's founder, Alfred Heber Holbrook.

☛ High Museum of Art. When the High Museum opened as the Atlanta Art Association in 1926, its collection was small enough to fit inside the donated Peachtree Street home of Mrs. Joseph M. High. As the collection grew, it was clear that a larger facility was needed. In 1979, thanks in part to a generous $7.5 million donation by Coca Cola head Robert M. Woodruff, the current museum site was built as part of the Woodruff Arts Center on Peachtree Street. The sleek, white postmodernist building, designed by architect Richard Meier, was hailed by the American Institute of Architects as one of the "ten best works of American architecture of the 1980s." Today, the museum has nearly 94,000 square feet of exhibit space, which houses a permanent collection containing 11,000 works of 19th- and 20th century American and European art, as well as contemporary and folk art.

☛ Michael C. Carlos Museum of Art. The largest collection of ancient Egyptian, Greek and Roman artifacts anywhere in the southeast resides at this museum on the campus of Emory University. Among the highlights are the mummy of Tahat, a first-century Buddha sculpture from India; and a fourth-century statue of Terpsichore, the Greek muse of dance. In 1999, the museum purchased several Egyptian antiquities from the Niagara Falls Museum, including a mummy whose identity was then unknown. When museum officials and Emory University scientists discovered that it was the pharaoh Ramesses I, the museum returned the mummy to Egypt as a gesture of goodwill.

☞ Morris Museum of Art. Located on the Riverwalk in downtown Augusta, the museum was the first in the U.S. to be entirely dedicated to Southern art. Its exhibits include portraits dating back to before the Civil War. Works on display were all created by artists who were either born in the South (such as Augusta native Jasper Johns) or influenced by it.

Sherman's March—Caught on Film

At a time when photography was still a relatively new art form, George N. Barnard used his lens to document key moments in the Civil War. As official photographer of the Military Division of the Mississippi, he captured Sherman's March to the Sea in a series of more than 60 photos, titled Photographic Views of Sherman's Campaign.

Lady of the Quilt

She could neither read nor write, so she told her stories in stitches. Harriet Powers began life in 1837 as a slave in rural Georgia, but she gained recognition as one of the greatest African American quilt makers in history. Her first story quilt, which depicted Biblical scenes on 299 separate pieces of cloth, caught the attention of a woman named Jennie Smith, who purchased it for $5. Today, the quilt is on display at the Smithsonian Institution in Washington, DC. A second quilt is displayed in the Museum of Fine Arts in Boston.

Comic Book Hero

Snobs may scoff that comic book illustrations aren't really art, but anyone who has taken a look at Jack Davis' considerable portfolio will argue otherwise. Born in Atlanta on December 2, 1924, Davis got his first lucrative illustrating job in 1949, working on a Coca Cola manual. He went on to create memorable cartoons for EC horror comics and *MAD Magazine*, as well as posters for Woody Allen's movie *Bananas* and the TV show *Get Smart*. The National Cartoonists Society named Davis Cartoonist of the Year in 2000.

An Artistic Legacy

Lamar Dodd was so talented as a child that he jumped straight from sixth grade into college art classes at the tender age of 12. The only caveat was that the school was LaGrange Female College, but Dodd was so committed to his art that he seemed not to mind being the odd man out in a classroom full of women. He channeled his intensity into a career in which he rose to become one of the most influential Southern artists of his time. Although most of his subjects dealt with everyday life, some of his best-known works were out-of-this-world depictions of space exploration that he created for NASA in the 1960s and '70s. Dodd shared his vision with his students when he later taught at the University of Georgia, and he helped shape its art program into one of the most respected in the country. Just before Dodd's death on September 21, 1996, the University of Georgia named the Lamar Dodd School of Art in his honor.

Jasper Johns

The images in his paintings—maps, flags and targets—are familiar and mundane, yet somehow entirely new and unexpected. Jasper Johns was a Georgia boy, born in Augusta in 1930, who made his mark on the art world in New York. The pivotal moment in Johns' career came in 1955 when he dreamed that he had painted a large American flag. The next day, he did it. That painting was followed by several other variations on the flag. The Museum of Modern Art in New York was so taken with Johns' work that they bought three pieces and helped establish him as one of the greatest abstract expressionists of all time.

THE MUSIC SCENE

Bard of Savannah

He's been called America's greatest lyricist, and who can disagree, with songs such as "That Old Black Magic," "Jeepers Creepers," "Autumn Leaves," "Moon River" and "When a Man Loves a Woman" in his repertoire. Johnny Mercer was born in Savannah in 1909, and during the course of his songwriting career, he wrote or co-wrote more than 1000 tunes. When he died in 1976, Mercer was buried in Bonaventure Cemetery, with the titles of many of his most famous songs engraved on his memorial.

DID YOU  **KNOW?**

The Mercer House in Savannah that was the scene of the murder in the book and movie *Midnight in the Garden of Good and Evil*, was built by General Hugh W. Mercer, Johnny Mercer's great grandfather.

Dangerous Stretch of Road

On October 29, 1971, Duane Allman of the Southern rock band, the Allman Brothers, was riding his Harley Davidson along a Macon road when he lost control and hit the back of a large truck. He died a few hours later. Almost exactly the same day in the following year, band member Berry Oakley was riding his motorcycle just three blocks away from the site of Allman's accident when he hit a city bus and also died. Both men are buried at Rose Hill Cemetery in Macon.

In Harmony

Amy Ray and Emily Saliers (known collectively as the Indigo Girls) are known as much for their political activism as for their elegantly layered harmonies. The pop-folk duo met when they were kids at Laurel Ridge Elementary School in Decatur, and they began their musical collaboration while in high school. Today, with more than seven million albums sold and 20 years in the music business, the Indigo Girls are still touring and performing as passionately as ever.

Heavenly Voice

Her soaring soprano has been called a "force of nature," wrapping itself as nimbly around the operatic compositions of Wagner, Mozart and Strauss as it has around jazz standards, American spirituals and French chansons. Jessye Norman's talents have been recognized numerous times—she was the youngest recipient of the Kennedy Center Honor; she was named an honorary ambassador to the United Nations; and her hometown of Augusta named an amphitheater and plaza after her.

Athens Alternative Scene

It's no wonder *Rolling Stone* magazine dubbed Athens the "best college music town in the country," considering that the town has spawned the likes of R.E.M., the B-52s, and Widespread Panic. Here's the lowdown on the Athens music scene:

R.E.M.: They ruled the underground indie scene in the early 1980s before becoming one of the most famous alternative bands in history. R.E.M. started with four students at the University of Georgia (none of them actually graduated)—bassist Mike Mills, drummer Bill Berry, guitarist Peter Buck and lead singer Michael Stipe. Their first single, "Radio Free Europe," became a college radio staple, but it wasn't until the release of "Losing My Religion" in 1991 that the band became mega rock stars. R.E.M. was inducted into the Rock and Roll Hall of Fame in 2007.

DID YOU KNOW?

R.E.M.'s original name was Twisted Kites. Would they have been just as successful with that name? We'll never know, because in the summer of 1980, the band members flipped through a dictionary and randomly picked out the name R.E.M.

B-52s: It all started over a giant flaming rum drink at an Athens Chinese restaurant back in 1976. Fred Schneider, Kate Pierson, Keith Strickland, Cindy Wilson and Ricky Wilson each picked a straw, and by the end of the night they had formed the "world's greatest party band." Named not for the bombers, but for the slang word for the bouffant hairdos that elevated Kate and Cindy to new heights, the B-52s spawned such New Wave party hits as "Rock Lobster" and "Love Shack." Following a couple of major setbacks—the death of guitarist Ricky Wilson from AIDS in 1985 and the temporary departure of Cindy Wilson—the B-52s are back together today and still making albums.

SOUL MEN (AND WOMEN)

Sittin' on the Dock of the Bay

As a child in Macon, Georgia, Otis Redding won the local $5 talent shows so many times that he was finally banned from competing. In the '60s, he shot to fame with his songs "Mr. Pitiful" and "Try a Little Tenderness." Sadly, on December 10, 1967, when Redding was at the height of his career, he was killed when his twin engine Beechcraft crashed into Lake Monona, near Madison, Wisconsin. Shortly after Redding's death, "(Sittin' on) the Dock of the Bay" rose to the top of the charts. It was his only number one hit.

Godfather of Soul

He went by many names—"The Godfather of Soul," "The Hardest Working Man in Show Business" and "Soul Brother Number One"—but whatever people called him, James Brown was unquestionably a legend in the music world. As a child growing up in a tough Augusta neighborhood, Brown shined shoes and danced for money. He performed gospel songs in church before forming the band, James Brown and the Famous Flames, with whom he cut his first record, "Please, Please, Please" in 1956. Brown followed the song up with a string of classics such as "Papa's Got a Brand New Bag," "I Got You (I Feel Good)" and "Think." A true innovator, Brown's rhythmic gliding dance moves influenced a generation of performers, and his music laid the foundation for funk, rap and hip-hop. Despite run-ins with the law (he did time in the late 1980s for leading police on a drug-fueled chase through two states), Brown remained a soul icon. In 2006, at age 73, he died of congestive heart failure at Crawford Long Hospital in Atlanta.

The Genius

The man they called "the Genius" was born Ray Charles Robinson in Albany, Georgia, on September 23, 1930. Despite losing his sight to glaucoma at age seven, Charles' vision came in the form of music. His goal early on was to mimic his hero, Nat "King" Cole, but Charles ultimately pioneered his own signature sound—a blend of gospel, R&B, country and jazz. In a career that spanned some 58 years, Charles created unforgettable melodies: "I Can't Stop Loving You," "Hit the Road Jack" and the tribute to his home state, "Georgia on My Mind." And he earned 12 Grammy awards in the process. Just months after Charles' death in June 2004, the movie *Ray* was released, earning its star, Jamie Foxx, an Academy Award for his portrayal of the legendary singer/songwriter.

The Architect of Rock and Roll

Many have called him the "architect of rock and roll," and it's hard to dispute the title. When he was born in Macon, Georgia, in 1932, Little Richard was known by the name Richard Penniman. His family was dirt poor, and his father sold moonshine to earn extra money. Richard began singing gospel in the church, and by age 15 was performing with a minstrel show under the name Little Richard. He had a minor hit song, "Every Hour" in Atlanta, but his career really took off when he joined Specialty Records and charted a string of hits—"Tutti Frutti," "Long Tall Sally" and "Lucille"—that helped launch the rock and roll industry. Little Richard's on-stage persona was as big as his music; his raspy voice was accompanied by a flamboyant six-inch pompadour, eyeliner and sequined vests (he claims to have later influenced Prince's look and sound). In 1957, Little Richard suddenly left the music business to enter the seminary. He returned a few years later, and he still performs today.

DID YOU KNOW?

Early in his career, Little Richard led a band made up of keyboardist Billy Preston, the young soul singer James Brown, and a talented guitarist named Jimi Hendrix.

Midnight Train to Georgia

She was only seven when she took home top prize in the Ted Mack's Original Amateur Hour in 1952. Atlanta native Gladys Knight later joined up with a few Pips, and they hit it big with "Midnight Train to Georgia" in 1973, followed by "If I Were Your Woman" and "Neither One of Us." Today, Knight is still into her music, but she also loves her chicken and waffles. She and gospel music star Ron Winans opened a chain of restaurants in Atlanta serving the strange gastronomic combo. You want syrup with that?

COUNTRY LEGENDS

Considering that Georgia is smack dab in the middle of the South, it's no surprise that the state has had a string of country music stars. Here are just a few.

Streaking to the Top of the Charts

It was the '70s, and the latest inexplicable craze among college students was to strip down and run. Capitalizing on the popularity of the streaking fad, country singer Ray Stevens released "The Streak" in 1974, and it shot to the top of the charts. Stevens, who was born Harold Ray Ragsdale in Clarkdale on January 24, 1939, also had hits with silly little ditties such as "Harry the Hairy Ape," "Santa Claus Is Watching You" and "I Need Your Help, Barry Manilow," as well as his more serious number one hit, "Everything Is Beautiful."

Country Boy from Marietta

He might not wear a cowboy hat, but Travis Tritt is pure country—with a rock and roll edge. His first performance was at age four, singing "Everything Is Beautiful" at the Assembly of God Church in his hometown of Marietta. By age eight, Tritt had taught himself to play guitar, and he was writing songs by the time he was 14. To appease his parents, who thought music was no way to make a living, Tritt settled down with a wife and a 9-to-5 job in his early 20s, but neither lasted long. By 1989, he had returned to his true love. After playing honky-tonk clubs for a few years, Tritt signed a contract with Warner Records in Nashville. He's had a string of hits since then, including "Country Club" and "T R O U B L E."

She's in Love with the Boy Named Garth

She flew to the top of the charts with her soaring voice, and became one-half of country music's royal couple. Way before "How Do I Live" and "XXXs and OOOs" made her a household name, Monticello born Trisha Yearwood was a receptionist at MTM records and a demo singer for aspiring songwriters. She finally broke out on her own in the spring of 1991 with her first number one hit, "She's in Love with the Boy," and she's been on the rise ever since. When Yearwood was a struggling singer in Nashville, she caught the eye of Garth Brooks, who hired her as a backup singer. Eventually the attraction turned personal, and the two were married in December 2005.

MUSICAL TRANSPLANTS

Some musical legends weren't born in Georgia, but they've since made the state their home. Here are a few.

Sir Elton

He was born more than 4000 miles and an entire continent away in Middlesex, England, but today, pop icon Elton John considers Atlanta his home away from home. His 2004 album, *Peachtree Road* is an homage to his adopted city. Things weren't so peachy in 2006, though, when John filed a suit in Fulton County Court, complaining that tax assessors had gone too far when they appraised his 12,000-square-foot Peachtree Road condo at $4.6 million—a million more than what the singer thought it was worth.

Being Bobby Brown

For a while, it seemed that every time Atlanta residents opened a newspaper there was another story about the latest antics of local pop power-couple Whitney Houston and Bobby Brown. Their tumultuous marriage began in 1992, when the pair was still at the top of the charts, but by the late 1990s their music had taken a backstage to their behavior. Brown was in and out of jail over the years, and Houston alternated between standing by her man and arguing with him. The couple finally called it quits in 2006.

Annoying the Neighbors

Although many Atlanta residents love having the country music legend nearby, some of Kenny Rogers' neighbors haven't been so pleased. In 2005, Rogers purchased a 7.5-acre plot of land in the Atlanta suburb of Sandy Springs for $2.3 million, with plans to build a new home for himself, his wife Wanda and their twin sons, Justin and Jordan. But a few months into the project,

Rogers decided that the home was going to be too big and called it quits. Neighbors who had endured months of digging, granite blasting and tree removal weren't amused.

TLC

Lisa "Left Eye" Lopez was born in Philadelphia, but her music career took off when she moved to Atlanta at age 19 and teamed up with Tionne "T Boz" Watkins and Rozonda "Chili" Thomas to form the hip-hop act, TLC. The group sold more than 20 million albums and became one of the biggest bands of the 1990s. Always considered the craziest member of the trio, Lopez made headlines in 1994 for torching the $2 million mansion she shared with boyfriend and former Atlanta Falcons star, Andre Rison. She was sentenced to five years' probation. In 2002, as Lopez was preparing to record a solo album under the pseudonym NINA ("New Identity Not Applicable"), she was killed in a car accident in Honduras. Thousands turned up at the New Birth Missionary Baptist Church in Lithonia to pay their respects to the hip-hop diva.

ARCHITECTURAL ICONS

A Greek Revival

The streets of Georgia are lined with many Greek-inspired homes and official buildings, with their stately columns, gabled roofs and porticos. Charles B. Cluskey was among the most famous of the Greek revival architects in the nation. He created some of Georgia's most recognizable structures, including the Medical College in Augusta and the Governor's Mansion in Milledgeville. Cluskey briefly moved to Washington to create plans for renovating the White House, Capitol, and Patent Building, before returning to Georgia to oversee the rebuilding of St. Simons' Lighthouse. Sadly, he passed away in 1871 before the project was finished.

King of Bridges

If it hadn't been for a man named King, many Georgia residents would be wading their way to work today. Horace King became one of the preeminent covered bridge builders in the state, constructing an estimated 100 crossings over nearly every major river in Georgia, as well as several in neighboring states. Born a slave, King had a master named John Godwin, who was contracted to erect the first public bridge connecting Alabama and Georgia. Recognizing King's talent, Godwin treated him more like a partner than a slave and allowed him to oversee several major bridge building initiatives. Godwin ultimately gave King his freedom in 1846, and King always remained loyal to his friend. When Godwin passed away, King built a monument over his grave "in lasting remembrance of the love and gratitude he felt for his friend and former master." After King died in 1885, his own grave remained unmarked until 1978, when the Troup County Historical Society created a memorial to him, reading, "Horace King, Master Covered Bridge Builder."

Bruce and Morgan

Thomas Henry Morgan was one-half of the highly successful architectural firm, Bruce and Morgan. With partner Alexander C. Bruce, Morgan made his mark designing colleges, courthouses, churches and other public buildings in a combination of Romanesque revival, Queen Anne and Gothic revival architectural styles. Among their accomplishments were the Wigwam Hotel in Indian Springs, the main building at Agnes Scott College, and the Citizens and Southern National Bank Building.

Reaching to the Sky

John Wellborn Root was born in Lumpkin, Georgia, but he traveled to Chicago to partner with renowned architect, Daniel Hudson Burnham. Together, the pair helped reshape that city's skyline. When he returned to his home state, Root designed one of the most important buildings in Atlanta—the Equitable Building (later renamed the Trust Company of Georgia building) in 1890. By today's standards, the eight-story building is a bit stumpy, but back when it was built, it was monumental.

A Woman's Touch

At a time when architecture was a field dominated by men, two women rose to fame. Henrietta Dozier was the first female architect in Georgia and the first woman to graduate from an accredited architecture school in the South. She is credited with designing the Episcopal Chapel for the All Saints Episcopal Church in 1903 and the Southern Ruralist Building in Atlanta.

Following in her footsteps was Leila Ross Wilburn, who was born in Macon in 1885. Fresh out of college, Wilburn set off around the country, capturing some 5000 photographs documenting different architectural styles. When she returned to Georgia, she joined the architectural firm of Benjamin R. Padgett and Son as a trainee. Over the years, Wilburn designed many Craftsman-style homes in midtown Atlanta.

Neel Reid

There was a time when people knew they had made it when they could afford to buy one of Neel Reid's homes. Reid (together with former Columbia University classmate Hal Hentz) designed some of the most prestigious houses in Atlanta. His stately classical, Tudor and Georgian style mansions remain among the most prominent addresses in Buckhead and Midtown today. Tragically, Reid died of brain cancer at his Roswell home in 1926 when he was only 41 years old.

A Modern Atlanta

Architect John C. Portman is credited with literally transforming Atlanta's skyline in the 1970s. But in the late '60s when he first proposed building a hotel with a 22-story atrium and a revolving rooftop restaurant, his investors thought the plan was so crazy that they pulled out of the project. So determined to see his vision come to fruition, Portman pitched the idea to every major hotel chain in the country until he convinced Hyatt to sign on. Today the Hyatt Regency Hotel's flying-saucer-like top is a centerpiece of the Atlanta skyline. Portman went on to build the 73-story Westin Peachtree Plaza, a huge steel and glass cylinder that for a time was the tallest hotel in the world, as well as the 13-block Peachtree Center.

WRITING DOWN SOUTH

Brer Rabbit

When Joel Chandler Harris was a child, he delighted in listening to the animal tales and folklore of African American storytellers George Terrell, Old Harbert and Aunt Crissy. When he grew up and became a writer, Harris used those stories as his model for his Uncle Remus book series, which recounted the misadventures of Brer Rabbit and Brer Fox. One of the best-known tales was "The Wonderful Tar Baby Story," in which Brer Fox makes a person out of a lump of tar. When Brer Rabbit tries to speak to the tar baby and it doesn't respond, he begins to kick it and gets stuck. To this day, the term "tar baby" is used to describe a situation from which it is difficult to escape.

A Poet

Conrad Aiken's childhood in Savannah was idyllic. That is, until the winter that his father, prominent doctor William Ford Aiken, killed his wife and then shot himself. Young Conrad was sent to Cambridge, Massachusetts, to live with his aunt and uncle. He attended Harvard University, where he befriended fellow poet T.S. Eliot. Aiken's poems earned him a Pulitzer Prize, a National Book Award and the National Medal of Literature. In 1962, Aiken returned to Savannah to write in the house next door to his boyhood home. In March 1973, then Georgia Governor Jimmy Carter named him the state's official Poet Laureate. Aiken died a few months later, on August 17, 1973.

Erskine Caldwell

His works dealt with poverty and racial injustice, topics Erskine Caldwell learned quite a bit about while helping his father, a Presbyterian minister, assist the needy in rural Georgia. Caldwell was born on December 17, 1903, in the small town of White Oak. In his early years, he hopped from job to job, taking turns as a cotton picker, bodyguard and professional football player, before deciding on a writing career. Caldwell ultimately wrote almost 150 short stories and more than 35 books, among the most famous of which were *Tobacco Road* (1932), *God's Little Acre* (1933) and *Trouble in July* (1940). After Caldwell died on April 11, 1987, the small white clapboard home in which he grew up was moved three miles down the road to nearby Moreland and transformed into a museum of his memorabilia.

A Lonely Hunter

Carson McCullers was born Lula Carson Smith on February 19, 1917, in Columbus. She began writing at age 16, modeling her early works after her literary hero, Eugene O'Neil. Just a few years later, McCullers developed her own literary voice and wrote her most influential novel, *The Heart Is a Lonely Hunter* (1940), a story about loneliness and isolation in a Southern town. She followed it up with *The Ballad of the Sad Café* and *The Member of the Wedding*. Four of her novels were turned into movies, and one, *The Member of the Wedding*, became a successful Broadway play. Plagued by illness throughout her life, McCullers died in 1967. She was posthumously inducted into the Georgia Women of Achievement in 1994.

The Color Purple

The story of Celie, a poor black woman struggling to escape from the oppressive men in her life and discover her identity in early 1900s rural Georgia, made author Alice Walker a household name and earned her a Pulitzer Prize for Fiction and a National Book Award. In 1985, Steven Spielberg and Quincy Jones turned *The Color Purple* into a movie, which earned 11 Academy Award nominations. The book was also adapted into a hit Broadway musical.

Making History

Among the most notable historians of the 19th century was Savannah-born Charles Colcock Jones. He published nearly 100 books and articles in his day, including *Antiquities of the Southern Indians, Particularly of the Georgia Tribes* (1873), *The Dead Towns of Georgia* (1878) and *History of Georgia* (1883).

Frankly My Dear...

Atlanta-born author Margaret Mitchell had been fascinated with the Civil War as a child. While laid up with an ankle injury, she turned that fascination into one of the best-known and most-read books of all time, *Gone With the Wind*, which was published in 1936. The title came from the Ernest Dowson poem "Cynara": "I have forgot much, Cynara! Gone with the wind, / Flung roses, roses riotously with the throng." The movie, starring Clark Gable and Vivien Leigh, premiered at the Loew's Grand Theater in Atlanta on December 15, 1939, with Mitchell in attendance. In August 1949, while crossing the street near her home, Mitchell was hit by an off-duty cab. She died five days later and was buried in Atlanta's Oakland Cemetery. *Gone With the Wind* was her only published novel.

WHAT TO READ, LISTEN TO AND WATCH

With so many different media organizations operating in the state, it's impossible to get bored in Georgia. Here's a flip through the local newspapers and radio and TV dials.

Newspapers

Albany Herald
Americus Times-Recorder
Athens Banner-Herald
Atlanta Business Chronicle
Atlanta Jewish Times
Atlanta Journal-Constitution
Augusta Chronicle
Brunswick News
Cairo Messenger
Cherokee Tribune

Columbus Ledger-Enquirer
Dade County Sentinel
Gwinnett Gazette
Jackson Herald
Macon Telegraph
Marietta Daily Journal
Milledgeville Union Recorder
Savannah News
Toccoa Record
Valdosta Times

Radio Stations

News/Talk

> Atlanta—WGST (640 AM) and WSB (750 AM)
> Augusta—WGAC (580 AM)
> Columbus—WRCG (1420 AM)
> Gainesville—WDUN (550 AM)
> Rome—WRGA (1470 AM)

Music

> Albany—WKAK (104.5 FM)—Country
> Atlanta—WAQK (1380 AM)—Gospel
> Atlanta—WKLS (96.1 FM)—Rock
> Atlanta—WZGC (92.9 FM)—Mix
> Atlanta—WNNX (99.7 FM)—Modern rock

Atlanta—WWWQ (100.5 FM)—Top 40
Atlanta—WYAY (106.7 FM)—Country
Atlanta—WCLK (91.9 FM)—Jazz
Augusta—WAFJ (88.3 FM)—Christian contemporary
Austell—WAOS (1600 AM)—Spanish
Cartersville—WBHF (1450 AM)—Oldies
Conyers—WPBS (1050 AM)—Gospel
Dahlonega—WKHC (104.3 FM)—Country
Decatur—WATB (1420 AM)—Regional Mexican
Douglas—WDMG (99.5 FM)—Classic rock
Gainesville—WYAY (106.7 FM)—Country
Greensboro—WDDK (103.9 FM)—Adult contemporary
Newnan—WCOH (1400 AM)—Country
Rome—WQTU (102.3)—Top 40
Savannah—WEAS (93.1 FM)—R&B
Savannah—WAEV (97.3 FM)—Top 40
Statenville—WHLJ (97.5 FM)—Urban contemporary
Sylvester—WRXZ (106.1 FM)—Hip-hop
Valdosta—WAAC (92.9 FM)—Country
Warner Robins—WELV (102.5 FM)—Smooth jazz

TV Stations
ABC

Atlanta—WSB Channel 2
Augusta—WJBF Channel 6
Columbus—WTVM Channel 9
Macon—WPGA Channel 58
Savannah—WJCL Channel 22

CBS

Atlanta—WGLC Channel 46
Augusta—WRDW Channel 12
Columbus—WRBL Channel 3
Macon—WMAZ Channel 13
Savannah—WTOC Channel 11

FOX

Albany—WFXL Channel 31
Atlanta—WAGA Channel 5
Augusta—WFXG Channel 54
Macon—WGXA Channel 24
Savannah—WTGS Channel 28

NBC

Albany—WALB Channel 10
Atlanta—WXIA Channel 11
Augusta—WAGT Channel 26
Columbus—WLTZ Channel 28
Macon—WMGT Channel 41

PBS

Albany—WABW Channel 14
Atlanta—WGTV Channel 8, WPBA Channel 30
Augusta—WCES Channel 20
Chatsworth—WCLP Channel 18
Columbus—WJSP Channel 28
Dawson—WACS Channel 25
Macon—WDCO Channel 29
Savannah—WVAN Channel 9
Waycross—WXGA Channel 8

CW

Atlanta—WUPA Channel 69
Valdosta—WGVP Channel 44

Independent

Atlanta—WTBS Channel 17
Columbus—WYBU Channel 16
Cordele—WSST Channel 55

TV AND RADIO PERSONALITIES

Bargain Hunter

If it were up to Atlanta native Clark Howard, no one would pay full price—ever. On his radio show and TV news segments, Howard doles out advice on everything from buying cheap airline tickets to avoiding scams. Howard started out in the travel business in the early '80s, and when he finally sold his chain of travel agencies and retired in 1987, he was so loaded that he didn't need to penny pinch. But one day Howard was a guest on a local radio program when a caller asked for inexpensive travel tips, and the question launched an advice career. Since then, Howard's radio show has been syndicated on more than 200 stations, he's launched the Consumer Action Center, and he's written a series of books offering advice to help consumers "save more and spend less." Oh, and the one thing he says he will splurge for? Ben & Jerry's Caramel Fudge ice-cream.

 Before he began helping to make American Idols out of wannabe singers, Ryan Seacrest held the 7:00 PM-to-midnight slot on Star-94 FM in his hometown of Atlanta.

Still Hair Today

She's had more hairstyles during her 30-some years anchoring the local news than Imelda Marcos had shoes, but her changing image hasn't done anything to dissuade Monica Kaufman's loyal fans. When Kaufman arrived at WSB-TV Channel 2 in 1975, she became the first African American and the first woman to anchor a news show in the Atlanta market, and she's still the cornerstone of that station's nightly news broadcast today.

Morning Mix

Some people loved their bubbly banter, while others grabbed for the radio dial as soon as they heard Steve & Vicki's morning show on Star-94. Love them or hate them, there's no mistaking Steve & Vicki's success—they had the longest running radio show in the city. After 17 years, Steve & Vicki signed off in November 2007.

JOURNALISTS

Cherokee Nation

The Cherokee occupied Georgia long before white settlers moved in. But by the 1800s, they were fighting for control over their land, which eventually led to a struggle within their own ranks. In 1828, the Cherokee Nation launched its own newspaper, the *Cherokee Phoenix*, with editor Elias Boudinot (born Gallagina "Buck" Watie) at the helm. At a time when whites were trying to push the Cherokee out of Georgia, Boudinot openly declared that the only way for his tribe to survive was to leave Georgia and relocate to U.S. government lands in the West. His position was an unpopular one with his people, particularly with Cherokee Nation chief John Ross, who wanted the Cherokee to remain right where they were. On August 11, 1832, Boudinot was forced to resign his position at the newspaper because of his dissenting opinions. In 1839, after thousands of Cherokee died during their forced march west on the Trail of Tears, supporters of Ross attacked Boudinot and stabbed him to death.

Spokesman of the New South

In 1874, while working as the Georgia correspondent for the *Atlanta Daily Herald*, a young journalist named Henry W. Grady caught the attention of bigwigs at the *Atlanta Constitution*, who offered Grady one-quarter ownership of the paper and a position as its managing editor. Grady turned the paper into a platform for his political views, publishing a number of editorials outlining his vision for a post Civil War "New South" driven by industry. After Grady's death in December 1889, both a county and a local hospital were named in his honor.

Newspaperwoman

World War II was a time of opportunity for many women in the workforce. For Celestine Sibley, a new reporter at the *Atlanta Constitution*, the drop in male employees allowed her to become one of the first female editors at the paper. Between 1941 and 1999, Sibley wrote 10,000 columns. Her last column appeared in the *Constitution* on July 25, 1999, just three weeks before she died.

The South's Conscience

Ralph McGill once told a group of schoolchildren that he had become a journalist "just because I needed a job." Yet despite his initial indifference, he became one of the most influential journalists in Georgia's history. As editor of the *Atlanta Constitution* from the '40s through the '60s, McGill's vehement opposition of segregation earned him a reputation as the "conscience of the South." In 1958, he was awarded the Pulitzer Prize for editorial journalism. Two years later, when McGill turned 62, the paper named him its new publisher. Despite not knowing how to run a paper from the ground up, McGill took the job in order to avoid the company's mandatory retirement age. He died of heart failure in Atlanta on February 3, 1969.

DID YOU KNOW?

You've heard of the *Atlanta Journal-Constitution*, but what about the *Great Speckled Bird*? Founded by Emory University students in the late '60s and named for a folk song performed by Roy Acuff, it became one of the longest-running underground papers of its time.

GREAT ENTERTAINERS

Another Fine Mess

One-half of what was arguably the most famous comedy team in history was born in Harlem, Georgia, in 1892. Oliver Hardy started out behind the scenes in movie houses and vaudeville, but became famous when he teamed up with British comedic actor Stan Laurel. The two were perfect opposites—Hardy was fat and bossy, and Laurel was skinny and naïve—differences that led them into many a foible and always caused Hardy to exclaim, "That's another fine mess you've gotten me into!" Between 1927 and 1940, Laurel and Hardy made 60 movies for Hal Roach Studios, including *The Second Hundred Years, Big Business* and *Sons of the Desert*. The duo was so inseparable that when Hardy died in 1957, Laurel swore he'd never perform again (despite many offers, he kept to his word.) Today, Harlem commemorates its favorite funny boy with a museum and an Oliver Hardy Festival held the first Saturday of every October.

Southern Belle in Hollywood

If things had turned out differently, Savannah native Miriam Hopkins might have been the recipient of that famous line, "Frankly my dear, I don't give a damn," instead of Vivian Leigh. Although she was beat out for the Scarlett O'Hara role in *Gone With the Wind*, Hopkins had an impressive film career nonetheless. She made a name for herself in movies such as *Dr. Jekyll and Mr. Hyde* in 1931 and *Becky Sharp* in 1935. Hopkins died in 1972, just days before her 70th birthday.

Hollywood Power Couple

Before there was "Brangelina," Paul Newman and Joanne Woodward were Hollywood's "It" couple. Woodward was born in Thomasville on February 27, 1930. A big film fan from the time she was a little girl, Woodward accompanied her mother to the Atlanta premiere of *Gone With the Wind*. When Vivian Leigh's limo pulled up, Woodward hopped right in, and onto the lap of a startled Laurence Olivier, who never forgot the incident. Once she graduated from college, Woodward began acting in earnest, but an acting coach advised her to lose the southern drawl or she'd never get cast. She did get cast, however—many times—and in 1952, she was introduced to a handsome young actor named Paul Newman. Although Newman was smitten at first glance, Woodward played hard to get, but the pair ultimately teamed up both on- and off-screen. They were married in 1958, and bucking the Hollywood trend, they've stayed together all these years.

Ossie Davis

When Davis was born in rural Cogdell, Georgia, the county clerk misheard his mother's dialectical pronunciation of his initials, R.C., and mistakenly registered him as "Ossie." The name stuck. Ossie Davis became not only a legend of stage and screen, but he was also a tireless civil rights activist. He starred in dozens of movies, including *The Joe Lewis Story* and Spike Lee's *Do the Right Thing*. Davis was also a regular on the television shows *The Cosby Show* and *Evening Shade*. Not willing to be limited by any one medium, Davis also wrote (he penned the Broadway musical "Purlie Victorius") and directed (he was behind the camera for the film *Cotton Comes to Harlem* in 1970). Both Davis and his wife, actress Ruby Dee, were honored many times for their work. President Clinton awarded them the National Medal of Arts in 1995 and the Screen Actors Guild granted them its Life Achievement Award in 2000. Davis died on February 4, 2005, at the age of 87.

DID YOU KNOW?

Ossie Davis delivered the eulogy at the funerals of both Malcolm X and Martin Luther King Jr.

You Might be a Redneck if...

"...you've been on television more than five times describing what the tornado sounded like."

"...you've ever cut your grass and found a car."

"...you've ever been too drunk to fish."

Long before his redneck routine made him a household name, Atlanta native Jeff Foxworthy was working in the computer industry when he entered a contest at a comedy club and won the top prize. His successful comedy career and a line of books, CDs, calendars and greeting cards transformed Foxworthy from a mere stand-up comic into a multi-millionaire. In 2007, he stopped pondering whether people were rednecks and started asking whether they were "Smarter than a 5th Grader" as host of the Fox Network's hit game show.

The Grin that Launched a Career

Open up the Campbell High School yearbook circa 1985 and you'll see a picture of a girl with an unmistakable ear-to-ear grin. Before she was *Pretty Woman*, Julia Roberts was just another kid growing up in the Atlanta suburb of Smyrna. But she had bigger and better things planned. At age 17, she left home for New York to pursue her acting career, and it paid off—big time. In 2007, Forbes put Roberts at number six on its list of the "20 Richest Women in Entertainment," with an estimated net worth of $140 million.

From Hollywood to Georgia

Rita Hayward started out her life in New York and became famous in L.A., but she's spending the rest of eternity in Georgia. The Hollywood starlet rose to fame in such movies as *Reap the Wild Wind* with John Wayne, and *I Want to Live!* for which she earned a Best Actress Oscar. Hayward eventually moved to Carrolton to be with her husband, Eaton Chalkley, and when she died in 1975, she was buried next to Chalkley in a local cemetery. Her gravestone reads simply "MRS. F.E. CHALKLEY," but the church added her famous name for the benefit of visitors.

HOLLYWOOD LOCAL

Movie Industry

L.A. isn't the only place to make movies, as filmmakers proved time and time again when they set their scenes in Georgia. Here are just a few of the movies and TV shows that have been filmed here:

Deliverance
Year: 1972
Stars: Jon Voight, Burt Reynolds, Ned Beatty, Ronny Cox
Plot synopsis: Four professionals from Atlanta take a weekend canoeing trip and end up "squealing like a pig."
Locations: Tallulah Gorge and the Chattooga River dividing Georgia and South Carolina
Fun facts: To save money, locals were cast as the creepy hill people.

Roots (TV miniseries)
Year: 1977
Stars: LeVar Burton, Ed Asner, Louis Gossett Jr., Vic Morrow, John Amos, Cicely Tyson, Maya Angelou
Plot synopsis: A historical drama chronicling the story of Kunta Kinte, an American slave, and several generations of his family.
Locations: Savannah and St. Simons Island
Fun facts: Roots became the highest-rated miniseries in history.

Smokey and the Bandit
Year: 1977
Stars: Burt Reynolds, Sally Field, Jackie Gleason
Plot synopsis: Bo "Bandit" Darville (Reynolds) makes a bet that he can make it from Georgia to Texas and back within 48 hours to pick up a 400-case shipment of beer. Along the way, he picks up Carrie (Field) and gets into a high-speed police chase.
Locations: McDonough and Jonesboro

Fun facts: Jackie Gleason reportedly modeled his character after Burt Reynolds' father, a Georgia sheriff. One of his trademark phrases was "sum bit" ("son of a bitch").

The Dukes of Hazzard (TV show)
Year: 1979–85
Stars: Tom Wopat, John Schneider, Catherine Bach
Plot synopsis: The adventures of two good old boys, Bo and Luke Duke, who continually tried to foil the scams of J.D. "Boss" Hogg in fictional Hazzard County, Georgia.
Location: Covington, Georgia (after the first five episodes, filming moved to a Warner Brothers set in Burbank, California)
Fun facts: More than 300 different "General Lee" cars were created for the show.

In the Heat of the Night (TV show)
Year: 1988–95
Stars: Carroll O'Connor, Howard E. Rollins Jr.
Plot synopsis: A sheriff and his police squad investigate crimes in the fictional town of Sparta, Mississippi.
Locations: Conyers, Covington
Fun facts: In the second season, the location looked a bit different. That's because the first season was filmed in Hammond, Louisiana, and then the show was moved to Georgia.

Driving Miss Daisy
Year: 1989
Stars: Morgan Freeman, Jessica Tandy, Dan Aykroyd
Plot synopsis: An elderly Jewish woman forms an unlikely friendship with her African American driver in 1950s-era Atlanta.
Locations: Atlanta and Decatur (Agnes Scott College served as one location)
Fun facts: Jessica Tandy won an Academy Award for her portrayal of Daisy Werthan. At 81, she was the oldest woman ever to win a Best Actress Oscar.

Glory

Year: 1989
Stars: Matthew Broderick, Denzel Washington, Cary Elwes, Morgan Freeman
Plot synopsis: The story of Colonel Robert G. Shaw and the first all-black volunteer company during the Civil War.
Locations: Jekyll Island and Savannah
Fun facts: The party scenes were filmed at the Mercer House in Savannah, which was also the setting for the movie *Midnight in the Garden of Good and Evil.*

My Cousin Vinny

Year: 1992
Stars: Joe Pesci, Ralph Macchio, Marisa Tomei, Fred Gwyne
Plot synopsis: Two "utes" get pinned for murder while driving through Alabama and call in the services of a New York personal injury lawyer who barely passed the bar exam.
Locations: Alto, Covinton, Gainesville, Monticello
Fun facts: The courtroom scenes were actually filmed in a converted warehouse with a corrugated metal roof. It was a typical Georgia summer, and temperatures on the set soared to above 100°F.

We Are Marshall

Year: 2006
Stars: Matthew McConaughey, Matthew Fox, David Straithairn
Plot synopsis: After members of the Marshall University football team die in a plane crash, the team's new coach tries to rally the school's football program.
Location: Atlanta
Fun Facts: During the stadium scenes, hundreds of locals were hired to fill the stands. The empty seats were also filled in with blow-up dummies and computer-generated people.

Forrest Gump
Year: 1994
Stars: Tom Hanks, Robin Wright Penn, Gary Sinise, Sally Field
Plot synopsis: This multiple Academy Award–winning movie
follows the exploits of Forrest Gump through combat in
Vietnam, work on a shrimp boat and meetings with presidents
John F. Kennedy and Lyndon B. Johnson.
Location: Savannah
Fun facts: Chippewa Square, where Forrest's bench scenes were
filmed, didn't actually have any benches. A bench was brought
in for the shooting, and it now sits in the Savannah History
Museum.

UNFORGETTABLE PEOPLE

Baton Bob

If you're ever walking down the streets of midtown Atlanta and you spot a tall African American man wearing a tutu and twirling a baton, be sure to stop and say hello. Baton Bob (aka Bob Jamerson) is an Atlanta street performer who adopted his persona after the events of September 11, 2001, to "lift people's spirits." He's become so popular that *Atlanta* magazine has named Bob one of the city's top personalities.

The Flower Guy

Drive through the busy Buckhead intersection of Paces Ferry Road and Northside Drive in Atlanta on just about any afternoon and you're bound to see the man locals refer to as "the Flower Guy." His real name is Robert (he won't reveal his last name), and he reportedly wound up in Atlanta in 1977 when his motorcycle ran out of gas en route from South Carolina to a job in Alabama. He stuck around and got a job selling flowers for the Sunshine Floral Company, but when it closed up shop in the mid-1980s, Robert started his own business. If you ever pass by the Flower Guy's corner and want to buy a bouquet, it will set you back $10 for a dozen red roses and $15 for a dozen colored roses.

GOING BATTY

Brave Moments
The Braves weren't born in Atlanta—they came by way of Boston and Milwaukee—but they sure made their mark here. Here is a quick timeline of some highlights in Atlanta Braves history.

- 1966: The braves moved from Milwaukee to Atlanta and set up residence in Atlanta Stadium.

- April 8, 1975: Hank Aaron broke Babe Ruth's home-run record by hitting his 715th, against the Dodgers.

- 1975: Media mogul Ted Turner bought the Braves.

- 1982: Hank Aaron was inducted into the Baseball Hall of Fame.

- 1991–93: The Braves made it to the World Series three years in a row, but they didn't win any of them.

- 1995: The Braves finally won the World Series, making it their first such win in 38 years.

DID YOU KNOW?

Baseball in the early 1900s was a segregated sport. Because black baseball players couldn't play on the same teams as white players, they had their own league, and their own local team, called the Atlanta Black Crackers. Separate leagues existed until the late 1940s.

Hank Aaron Stats

This Atlanta Brave has gone down as one of the all-time greatest baseball players in history. Here are just a few of his amazing stats:

- ☞ 755 career home runs
- ☞ 2174 runs
- ☞ 3771 hits
- ☞ 2297 RBIs
- ☞ 6856 total bases

The Crackers

You've likely heard of the Atlanta Braves, but what about the Atlanta Crackers? Before the Braves moved to Atlanta from Milwaukee, the Crackers were the state's main baseball attraction. No one is exactly sure where the name of this minor league team originated—it might have come from the whips local farmers cracked to get their horses moving, or from the name of the city's previous team, the Firecrackers.

Whatever the source of the name, the Crackers were one of the most successful minor league teams in history, winning 17 Southern League championships between 1901 and 1965. In 1965, the Crackers played their final game in the newly constructed Atlanta Stadium, which became the home of the Braves the following year.

PASSING THE PIGSKIN

The Falcons Soar

In 1965, when the NFL awarded a football franchise to life insurance executive Rankin M. Smith for $8.5 million, Atlanta became home to the 15th NFL team in the country. Fans submitted suggestions for the team's name, and Miss Julia Elliott, a teacher from Griffin, Georgia, won. She wrote, "The falcon is proud and dignified, with great courage and fight."

And One Falcon Falls

Falcons quarterback Michael Vick was really in the doghouse in July 2007 when a federal grand jury in Richmond, Virginia, indicted him for running a dog-fighting ring out of his home in Virginia. In August, the NFL suspended him indefinitely, and on December 10, 2007, the sports star was sentenced to 23 months in jail. He was ordered to pay more than $900,000 as restitution for the dogs seized from his property. Once in federal prison, Vick can get his sentence reduced by 15 percent with good behavior.

"Mr. Falcon"

Tommy Nobis was the very first player to be drafted by the Falcons, and he made it to the Pro Bowl in his first year—a pretty significant accomplishment for a rookie. Nobis went back to the Pro Bowl four more times with his team, and he led the Falcons in tackles during 9 of his 11 seasons.

DID YOU  KNOW?

Although the Falcons took off in 1965, they didn't make it to the Super Bowl until 1998, when they faced off against the Denver Broncos. The Broncos won 34–19.

Trophy Man

When John Heisman took over as coach of the Georgia Tech football team in 1904, he was the first college football coach to ever earn a paycheck. He led the team through 16 winning seasons, including three undefeated seasons (1915–17) in a row and the record-breaking 1916 win over Tennessee's Cumberland University by a score of 222–0. When Heisman died in 1936, the Heisman Trophy—college football's top award—was named in his honor.

Go Bulldogs!

They've won five national championships, a dozen Southeastern Conference (SEC) titles and they've spawned the likes of Pro Football Hall of Famer Fran Tarkenton and Heisman Trophy winners Frank Sinkwich and Herschel Walker. Since their first kickoff on January 25, 1892, the University of Georgia's Georgia Bulldogs (or "Dawgs," as fans like to call them) have consistently been ranked among the leading college football teams in the nation.

Uga the Bulldog is the University of Georgia's official team mascot. Each new incarnation is given a different number (the current mascot is Uga VI). Probably the most famous of the pups was Uga V, who appeared in the movie *Midnight in the Garden of Good and Evil* and on the cover of *Sports Illustrated*.

BASKETBALL

Shoot Like a Hawk

The Atlanta Hawks have been an Atlanta sports institution since 1968, when the team relocated from St. Louis. After five years of sharing the Alexander Memorial Hall with the Georgia Tech basketball team, the Hawks moved to their own, bigger digs—the new 16,500-seat Omni arena—in 1972. Fans of the Hawks have gotten to watch some of the greatest stars in the history of the sport over the years, including Dominique Wilkins, Moses Malone, Dikembe Mutombo and legendary coach Lenny Wilkens.

The Human Highlight Film

Dominique Wilkins has made so many spectacular plays during his career that he's been dubbed the "Human Highlight Film." Born in Paris, France, Wilkins started making headlines while a student at the University of Georgia, where he averaged 21.6 points a game. The 6-foot 8-inch star played for the Atlanta Hawks from 1982 to 1994, until the team's managers shocked fans by trading their all-time leading scorer to the Los Angeles Clippers for Danny Manning. When he retired in 1999, Wilkins was ranked seventh on the all-time scoring list with 26,534 career points.

EVEN MORE SPORTS

It's Atlanta!

It all began with an idea: one day in the late '80s, the notion that Atlanta should host the Olympic Games hit attorney Billy Payne "like a bolt of lightning from the sky." To make his dream a reality, Payne had to raise $7.5 million and somehow convince the International Olympic Committee (IOC) that his city was worthy of the most important sporting event in the world. His efforts paid off in 1990, when the IOC announced that Atlanta had beaten out Athens, Belgrade, Manchester and Melbourne to host the 1996 Olympics. The city prepared by adding some 7500 hotel rooms and sprucing up its existing streets and parks.

The events kicked off on July 19, 1996, when boxing legend Muhammad Ali lit the torch at the opening ceremonies. About 11,000 athletes and an estimated two million visitors from 196 countries converged on venues across Atlanta and throughout the state.

Heavyweight

As a child growing up in Atlanta, Evander Holyfield dreamed of becoming an Atlanta Falcons star. Though he served admirably as offensive fullback and middle linebacker on the Warren Memorial Boy's Club team, Holyfield's curiosity eventually steered him onto another career path. After repeatedly trying to gain access to the restricted area of the Club, the boxing area, Holyfield eventually convinced the coach to let him in and allow him to join the boxing team. Even as a young man he was an impressive boxer, with a 169–11 record. By the early '80s Holyfield was a formidable opponent in the ring. He won a bronze medal at the 1984 Los Angeles Olympic Games, and in 1990 he became the Heavyweight Champion of the World when he defeated James "Buster" Douglas in three rounds. It's a title that he's held four times, beating even Muhammad Ali's record.

Golf Legend

The man who is considered to be the greatest amateur golfer in history never had any formal training. Instead, Bobby Jones picked up his signature swing by following around the golf pro at East Lake Country Club in Atlanta. His mimicry paid off. Between 1923 and 1930, Jones dominated the sport, winning 13 major golf championships and an unprecedented four major titles in a single season. Then in 1930, when he was at the top of his game, Jones shocked his fans by retiring from competitive play at just 28 years old. Though he didn't play professionally again, Jones remained active in the golf world. Among his greatest accomplishments was creating the design for the Augusta National Golf Course, which hosts the Masters tournament each year.

Atlanta Motor Speedway

Today, the Atlanta Motor Speedway in Hampton is one of the best places in the country to watch racecars zoom by. Back in the '60s and '70s when it was called Atlanta International Raceway, the track wasn't nearly as impressive. Money was so tight that there was just one bathroom in the infield, and there were no stands—people used to bring blankets and sit in the dirt to watch races. Things changed in 1990 when Bruton Smith bought the place and changed the name to Atlanta Motor Speedway. He expanded the seating capacity by 25,000, put in several luxurious suites and added the Busch Series, drag racing, Indy car racing and business conventions to the Speedway's repertoire.

Million Dollar Bill

Bill Elliott's father once said that he got his boys into racing to keep them off the back roads. Elliott quickly proved he had talent on the track, regularly whizzing by his competitors on the way to the finish line at Dixie Speedway near his home in Dawsonville. Racing was always a family affair, with Elliott's dad as owner, his brother Ernie as crew chief and his other brother Dan as transmission builder. In 1985, after winning the Daytona 500, the Winston 500, and the Southern 500 earned him a hefty $1 million bonus, Elliott was nicknamed "Million Dollar Bill." He has been one of the top-earning drivers throughout his career, bringing home an estimated $73 million over 44 wins.

TEN GOOD REASONS TO LIVE IN GEORGIA

10. If someone tells you to "take a hike," you'll have no problem following their orders. Georgia has more than 100 different hiking trails.

9. When it comes to eating out, no one will nag you about your diet while you fill your face with great barbecue, fried catfish, Vidalia onions and country caviar (aka boiled peanuts).

8. It is the biggest state east of the Mississippi and is so large that you could fit Connecticut, New Jersey, Rhode Island, Massachusetts and Vermont inside it and still have room to spare.

7. Even when the mercury soars past the century mark, you don't have to break a sweat, because just about every building is perfectly climate-controlled.

6. You can use phrases such as "I'm fixin' to" and "I might could," and everyone will know exactly what you're talking about.

5. Despite being nowhere near the coast, Atlanta is home to the "eighth ocean of the world"—the Georgia Aquarium.

4. Serious about your sports? Not a problem. Football, basketball, hockey, NASCAR—they're all well represented here.

3. You can wear short sleeves in the middle of January, and the kids can still have the occasional snowball fight.

2. No matter what year it is, the antebellum South and the Civil War are still alive.

1. There must be something to like about Georgia, because people are coming here in droves. The population has been rising at more than twice the national average.

ABOUT THE AUTHORS

Stephanie Watson

A passionate reader from an early age, Stephanie Watson devours books. Her kindergarten teacher initially noted that she didn't skim books for the pictures, but actually read them, too! That love of reading led to her current career as freelance writer. Stephanie's work has been seen or heard on TV, radio, the web, newspapers and in a number of published books. A resident of Smyrna, Georgia, she enjoys spending time with her young son and giving back to the community through work as the chair of a charity organization.

Lisa Wojna

Lisa is the co-author of at least 12 trivia books, as well as being the sole author of five other non-fiction books. She has worked in the community newspaper industry as a writer and journalist and has traveled all over the world. Although writing and photography have been a central part of her life for as long as she can remember, it's the people behind every story that are her motivation and give her the most fulfilment.

THE ILLUSTRATORS

Patrick
Hénaff

Roger
Garcia

Peter
Tyler

Roly
Wood